A STRONG DELUSION

JOE DALLAS

HARVEST HOUSE PUBLISHERS
Eugene, Oregon 97402

Cover by Koechel Peterson & Associates, Minneapolis, Minnesota

A STRONG DELUSION

Copyright © 1996 by Harvest House Publishers
Eugene, Oregon 97402

Library of Congress Cataloging-in-Publication Data

Dallas, Joe, 1954–
    A strong delusion / Joe Dallas.
       p. cm.
    Includes bibliographical references.
    ISBN 1-56507-431-9 (alk. paper)
       1. Homosexuality—Religious aspects—Christianity—Controversial literature. 2. Homosexuality in the Bible. 3. Homosexuality—Biblical teaching. 4. Dallas, Joe, 1954– . I. Title.
BR115.H6D36 1996
261.8'35766—dc20   96-14509
                                 CIP

Printed in the United States of America.

03 04 05 06 07 08 09 / BC / 14 13 12 11 10 9 8 7 6

To the leadership of
Exodus International—

KEEP STANDING

Contents

Introduction

I remember clearly, and with inexpressible regret, the day I convinced myself it was acceptable to be gay and Christian.

The local Metropolitan Community Church (a pro-gay denomination) was opening its morning service just as I slipped into a seat near the back. I had passed the church hundreds of times before, having been the associate pastor of a Foursquare church not three blocks away, and had always been intrigued at the thought of gays congregating as Christians.

"What do they do in there?" I'd chuckle to my friends when we would drive by the gay church. Then we would swap sarcastic guesses as to how homosexuals might try to reconcile their practices with Christianity.

That was years earlier, years when I could laugh at homosexuality, certain that my own struggles with it were over. The rigors of active ministry had buried the memories—the childhood molestation by strangers, the adolescent encounters with men from other cities—and I felt immune from sexual temptations.

My safety was precarious, though. One step into an adult bookstore was all it had taken to end my ministry and plunge me into a series of sexual excesses with both men and women, culminating in a year-long relationship with the owner of a gay bar. He was "committed" to another man; no matter, we'd meet every night after hours, and I'd drive home drunk at 4:00 A.M. I would then rise for work, exhausted and confused.

After finally breaking it off with him, I took a hard look at myself and what I had come to. I was 23 years old, and already I'd been ordained and defrocked. I had disgraced the ministry when my escapades came to light, and then committed adultery with the wife of a close friend—losing a child to abortion as a result. I had hired prostitutes, developed a two six-pack-a-day drinking habit, entered the gay community, and endured a nightmarish relationship. Now that I was alone again, life looked incredibly bleak.

So did my options. Repenting and returning to my old church seemed out of the question. I missed the fellowship of Christian friends, but I thought that they'd never take me back—and why should they, after the way I'd betrayed them? Yet the promiscuous, hard-driving lifestyle I had adopted was a dead-end as well. I wanted to indulge my sexual tastes, but not so wildly. I also wanted Christianity, but not without my sexuality. In short, I wanted it all, a common malady of the times.

So now it was desperation, rather than the intrigue I'd felt earlier, urging me to visit the Metropolitan Community Church that October morning of 1978. I wanted to see if it was possible to be actively homosexual, a Christian, and confident of a right standing before God.

I knew better, of course. I knew the scriptural condemnations of homosexuality in both the Old and New Testaments were clear and final; I knew that any attempt to get around them was purely self-serving. But it *was* self, after all, that I was serving in those days. Every major decision I had made that year—entering the pornographic bookstore, the adultery, the homosexuality—had been based on what *I* wanted, not on what was right. In that darkened frame of mind, I was ready to believe what I *wanted* to believe instead of what I *truly* believed. And what I wanted to believe, more than anything, was that my sexuality and faith could live together peacefully. In visiting the gay church, I was looking for something to confirm that belief.

The first confirmation came with the music. The choir opened the service with, of all things, an anthem by Bill and Gloria Gaither! I was caught short, then comforted, as the familiar melody washed over me. I relaxed a bit, then spotted a worship book in the pew. Opening it, I was delighted to find many of the solidly evangelical hymns and choruses I'd sung years ago. *With songs like these,* I reasoned, *this MUST be a Christ-centered church.*

People were singing along with the choir now, some even lifting their hands. If not for the name on the building, and the fact that some same-sex couples were linking arms, the service was shaping up to be like that of any conservative, mildly charismatic church.

I glanced sideways at the women and men around me. Until then my exposure to the gay community had been limited to what I'd seen in the bars—tight Levi's, muscle shirts, and foul behavior. Now I was confronted with a congregation full of moderate-looking gays and lesbians of all ages. None of them confirmed the stereotype so many people have of homosexuals. The men, by and large, dressed, spoke, and carried themselves normally; the women's manners were generally feminine. And so a second confirmation dawned on me: "gay" did not have to mean "sleazy" or "outlandish." These were normal looking people, leading respectable lives. My hopes grew—*maybe I could be one of them!*

Minutes later we were on our feet, singing and clapping through a string of upbeat choruses, when the most incredible feeling swept over me. My chest seemed to cave in, my eyes filled, and my legs buckled. It was the music. I was singing praises, something I thought I would never do again.

I had to sit down and weep. After a year of chaotic, utterly godless living, it felt so *good* to sing again—so blessed and familiar, like returning home from a war.

Something warm surged through me—something powerful, consoling, reassuring. *Just rest*, it seemed to say as I relaxed and let the tears flow. *Everything's going to be fine.*

By the time I pulled myself back together, the sermon had begun. The pastor's style was folksy, well suited to his hefty, rather jolly appearance. I liked him instantly, though within minutes I could see we were worlds apart theologically. His sermon included questionable ideas ("God gave us only two commandments: to love Him and to love each other. Everything else is fluff") and ludicrous statements ("I don't like the term 'Born Again.' I prefer to say we're recycled!"). But when he got on the subject of homosexuality and the church, my thoughts wandered in directions they'd never gone before.

"Gays have solidarity," he explained, "not so much because of who we are but because of how we're treated. There's no group in the country so reviled as us. And so slandered! Listen to almost any television preacher talk about us and you'll hear lies upon lies."

A bit of an exaggeration, I felt, but only a bit. The Anita Bryant campaign in Florida had recently triggered a national debate on homosexuality, and some preachers had jumped into it ill-prepared, throwing harsh rhetoric about gays over the airwaves. I shared the pastor's anger over that.

And yes, there *was* solidarity at this church; I recognized it as soon as I stepped into the sanctuary. Years earlier, I had been part of the youth revival known as the Jesus movement. We, too, had been maligned at times, ridiculed by a world that couldn't understand us. So I was familiar with the power of solidarity among a tight-knit group, and I missed it. I also missed having a cause, or a mission. *Might I find it with these people?*

"They condemn us," the pastor continued, "and call our love a sin. If that's what they truly believe, why don't they do anything to help us get over it?"

Nods and murmurs of agreement rippled through the congregation.

"Ask yourselves this," he challenged, pointing at all of us: "Could any of you, in the churches you grew up in, raise your hand during a prayer meeting and say, 'I'm homosexual and need help; please pray for me'?"

The very idea provoked an eruption of laughter. I joined in, knowing all too well the improbability of such a thing.

But why?

The thought stopped my laughter cold.

Why indeed? I had seen people request prayer in church for any number of problems—*sinful* problems, mind you, such as selfishness, lust, and bitterness—without raising eyebrows. Yet I'd known people in those same churches who would never have admitted a problem with homosexuality; the repercussions would have been unthinkable.

For that matter, I had heard testimonies, received by the church with enthusiasm, of people overcoming drug addiction, alcoholism, and immorality of all sorts. Except *this* sort.

This meant one of two things: either God delivered very few people from homosexuality or, more likely, those who were homosexual were too ashamed or intimidated to admit it.

But again, *why?* Why was homosexuality so unfairly, and so unbiblically, set apart as the "Unspeakable Sin"?

The question persisted. I felt a peculiar anger rising—the self-righteous ire of a victim. The pastor had touched a nerve.

"Perhaps," he mused, "it's a good thing your church *didn't* offer you help. If they had, it would only have fed the notion that you needed their so-called help for your so-called problem when, in fact, you *didn't!*"

Applause broke out.

"Because it *isn't* a problem!"

Whistles and shouts of "amen" sounded.

I hesitated to join in this time. It was one thing to indulge, rebelliously, in something you knew to be wrong;
saying the thing itself was not wrong was another matter. *That* required a radically changed mind-set.

But wasn't that what I had come for? I teetered over
the thought as he repeated himself: "It isn't a problem!"

Maybe it isn't, I thought, closing my eyes. *Please, let
it not be a problem. Please let this be true.*

"But because so many of us *think* it's a problem," he
continued, "because so many of us have been *told* it's a
problem, we've grown up hating ourselves."

He paused to let it sink in.

"Hating ourselves!" he stressed. "Hating the very core
of our being, the thing that defines us. Do you all know
what homophobia is?"

The verbal response indicated they certainly did.

"Do you think homophobia is something only the
bigots feel?"

The question was rhetorical; no one answered this
time.

"It's right here!" he snapped, thumping his chest.
"Right in our *hearts!* We swallow their lies, we believe
we're perverts, so we *act* like perverts! No wonder so
many of us have been promiscuous! No wonder so many
of us have lived half our lives getting drunk in bars, or
high on drugs, or prowling in bathhouses. When you've
been oppressed, when you've been told all your life
you're the rottenest kind of sinner, you believe it! *That's*
why there's so much self-destructive behavior in our
community!"

I was startled to hear an "amen!" leap out of me, but
that didn't stop me from repeating it, louder and
stronger.

It wasn't my fault, I marveled.

"Amen!"

*The sleeping around, the abortion, the craziness—I
was only acting out the role society had cast me in.*

"Amen!"

THEY were wrong, not me. They LIED to me. They— what was the word he used?—they OPPRESSED me!

"Amen!"

The confirmation I wanted lay in that single word. I was *oppressed*—all gays were *oppressed*. *Oppression* was responsible for my misconduct.

I could forgive myself now. The thought drew fresh tears.

I could forgive myself, and move in another direction with a new identity—as a gay Christian.

It was oddly liberating to put the two words together.

Gay Christian. Homosexual, but sexually *responsible*, not promiscuous. A God-fearing, churchgoing gay man with a cause: To combat homophobia and the oppression of all gay people.

The idea thrilled me. A cause—something to live for, to fight for.

The pastor's next words seemed to have been spoken just to me: "But Jesus said the truth would set us free. And hasn't it? Hasn't learning the truth—that God loves you just as you are, that He doesn't condemn you, that Jesus died not just for the heterosexual but for the homosexual as well—hasn't that truth liberated you?"

When the applause died down, he added: "And doesn't that compel you to take that liberation everywhere? To tell our people they *can* be gay and Christian? And to stand up to the fundamentalists and say *No More! God is our God, too!*"

Yes, I agreed, swept up in his passion along with the others. His words struck a defiant chord in me. I laughed and clapped and repeated *yes it does* over and over. It was exhilarating.

When the mood finally settled again, I looked around me and smiled, mentally forming a decision: *This is what I was looking for; this is where I could have it all. These people—gay and Christian—could be my people. I could belong here.*

Even as I considered it, I was flooded with peace.

The pastor ended his sermon. Now staff members joined him to prepare the altar for communion. I couldn't wait. Taking the Lord's Supper, I felt, would initiate me into this group, and I was more than ready.

"Behold the Lamb of God," he announced shortly, holding the host and chalice in the air as the staff lined up to serve the elements. "The table is prepared. Come."

Randomly, people began leaving their seats. I was starting to leave mine when a torrent of doubt slammed into me.

Joe, what on earth are you about to do? I thought. I froze halfway out of my seat.

It was my early training, my years of Bible study and sound teaching, posing the question, trying to dissuade me from a lethal decision. Because I knew, somehow, that if I stepped into that aisle and took communion—in *that* church, with *those* beliefs—I would seal a commitment that would take years, perhaps a lifetime, to reverse. Was this really what I wanted?

I settled back into the pew, shaken, just as another question presented itself: *What about the Bible?* I touched my forehead and noticed I had broken into a sweat.

This gay pastor had indicted the church for misunderstanding homosexuals. But did that justify homosexuality itself? Suppose he was right: suppose gays *had* a legitimate beef against society. Suppose Christians *did* need to be more loving toward homosexuals. Suppose some preachers *were* too harsh when referring to the subject. Did that make all the biblical injunctions against homosexuality null and void?

My discomfort was growing by the minute.

All my Christian life I had known the importance of judging everything by Scripture, not feelings. Not once, I noted, did this man back his assertion that homosexuality is okay in God's sight with any biblical support—because, of course, there was none. And if there was none, the argument was settled. No matter how peaceful, exhilarated, or relieved I had felt earlier, feelings would not, *could* not, make something wrong into something right.

I slumped forward, deflated.

That last point was inarguable, but I was not willing to accept it—not having just found some relief from the inner turmoil I had suffered for 12 endless months. My mind raced for a rebuttal, something to bring back the peace I'd known minutes earlier, when an entirely new line of thought occurred to me: Even if it *wasn't* right, was it so terribly wrong?

I clutched the idea, toying with it.

Compared to drinking and carousing, wasn't the life I was considering at least an improvement? I would be in church again, after all, singing and praying with people whose standards were much higher than those of the bar crowd I'd been running with. Surely God approved of what could only be called a step in the right direction.

Just then a couple of handsome, well-dressed young men passed my seat, arms entwined, moving toward the communion table.

Look at them! I chided myself, watching them kneel and hold hands, sharing the bread and wine. They were so serene, beaming health and prosperity. *They're not worrying about a few little Bible verses; why should you? Besides, look at the songs we're singing, and the way everyone is worshiping. All these gay and lesbian Christians are obviously devoted to God and are comfortable with themselves, so what's your problem?*

Some peace trickled back; *that* kind of thinking definitely felt better. I scanned the congregation, most of them making their way to the altar, singing or humming quietly along with the organist. They all looked so content, so free of turmoil over their sexual behavior. If I would only give up my letter-bound obsession with the Bible, I would be content, too. And I would be comfortable with myself, like them; didn't that count for something?

I closed my eyes and sighed, knowing I had just hit the bottom-line issue: a contest between comfort and truth. I could either believe what made me *comfortable*, or I could believe what I knew to be *true*. Never had the choice been clearer; to this day, I am amazed at how easily I made it.

I would do it. I would go to the altar, receive communion, and take my place with my gay brothers and sisters. I would join this church, this ideology, and make it my own. My life would again serve a purpose. I could already envision myself as an activist. It was the logical thing to do, I assured myself, and it was right. And even if it wasn't right, I would learn to live with it.

With that in mind, I opened my eyes, stood tall, and stepped into the aisle.

The "Gay Christian" Movement

Today, the Christian church must seriously consider the thousands of men and women who are likewise stepping into the aisles, away from biblical standards, into the strong delusion of the "gay Christian" movement.[1] If mine were an isolated case, there'd be no need to concern ourselves with it. But in the years since I left the gay church and lifestyle in 1984, I've seen my story repeated too many times, in too many lives. It's time the church recognized those lives, and the seductive effect the gay Christian movement is having on them.

Webster refers to a movement as a "tendency, a trend, or a series of organized activities working toward an objective." The gay Christian movement meets all three of Webster's qualifications: it represents a *tendency* among Christians who are homosexually tempted, to yield to that temptation and then try to justify it. It represents an ongoing *trend* within parts of the Christian church to legitimize homosexual behavior. And it's brimming with *organized activities working toward an objective* of widespread acceptance of homosexuality in both the church and society.

The gay Christian movement is much like the broader gay rights movement in that it seeks legitimization (not just tolerance) of homosexuality. Gay spokesmen have made no secret of the fact that this is their goal. Activist Jeff Levi put it plainly to the National Press Club during the 1987 Gay Rights March on Washington:

> We are no longer seeking just a right to privacy and a protection from wrong. We also have a right—as heterosexual Americans already have—to see government and society affirm our lives. Until our relationships are recognized in the law—in tax laws and government programs to affirm our relationships, then we will not have achieved equality in American society.[2]

But the gay Christian movement takes it a step further by redefining homosexuality as being God-ordained and morally permissible:

> I have learned to accept and even celebrate my sexual orientation as another of God's good gifts.
>
> —Gay author Mel White[3]

> How could we go on being ashamed of something that God created? Yes, God created homosexuals and homosexuality.
>
> —Reverend Troy Perry, founder, Metropolitan Community Church[4]

> I offered thanks to God for the gift of being gay.
>
> —Gay priest Malcom Boyd[5]

When God is alleged to sanction the abominable, a religious travesty is being played out, and boldly. The travesty is twofold. Not only are believers falling into homosexual sin and legitimizing it; scores of heterosexual Christians are applauding them as they do! Prominent religious figures and Christian organizations are giving a friendly nod to gay ideology, making Isaiah's famous warning more relevant than ever: "Woe unto them that call evil good, and good evil; that put darkness for light, and light for darkness" (Isaiah 5:20 KJV).

To squelch any doubt about the prevalence of darkness being called light *among professing Christians*, consider the following examples:

• A former pastor, seminarian, and ghostwriter for Billy Graham, Jerry Falwell, Pat Robertson, and Oliver North is now openly gay and is committed to convincing both church and society that homosexuality is a gift from God, and that the "Religious Right" is wrong in condemning gay behavior.[6] His book, which promotes this philosophy, was endorsed by an evangelical best-selling author and editor for *Christianity Today* magazine.[7]

• The composer of one of the most beloved gospel songs of the past three decades is now openly lesbian—attending, writing, and performing music for the largest pro-gay denomination in the country.[8]

• The former co-host of what was once the nation's most popular Christian television program, who has produced numerous Christian books and recordings, is now co-hosting a secular entertainment talk show with a man who openly declares himself to be gay and Christian.[9]

• A handful of American Baptist churches in Northern California have adopted policies openly affirming homosexual relationships, leading to their expulsion from the American Baptist Convention. When commenting on criticism of their pro-gay views, one Baptist pastor remarked, "If two people of the same sex want to have sex, it's none of my business if they are committed to each other and follow the same standards the church has set for heterosexual couples."[10]

• A popular gospel artist, who frequently performs at conservative Christian events and churches, is also a defender of the pro-gay religious movement. Though heterosexual, he endorses the notion that homosexuality is legitimate, and lends his talents to meetings of "gay Christian" groups.[11]

• When a spokesman for the Salvation Army in San Francisco described homosexuality as "a serious threat to society as a whole," the San Francisco board of supervisors voted to withhold federal funding from the group. Salvation Army officials scurried to correct the "problem," dismissing their spokesman's remarks as "outdated" and promising to implement "sensitivity-training programs."[12]

Compounding the problem are the denominations that, despite their official positions on homosexuality, are reconsidering the matter or allowing their members to ignore their stated policies on sexual conduct. A confused believer does not have to visit a "gay church," as I did, for affirmation of his homosexuality. Several Protestant bodies contain both leaders and parishioners who fully embrace the pro-gay position, even as the denominations technically reject it.

A curious mixture is brewing in Christendom. Major denominations may be filled with women and men committed to biblical integrity, yet a pro-gay contingent has been allowed to flourish alongside them. So, when a homosexual person seeking truth enters a mainline church, what might he find today?

In the Episcopal church, he might encounter some "progressive" bishops who have been ordaining openly homosexual priests for "decades—more than 100 since 1977, by some estimates."[13] In 1994, he'd learn, a number of Episcopal bishops signed a statement agreeing that homosexuality and heterosexuality are "morally neutral," that both "can be lived out with beauty, honor, holiness, and integrity," and those "who choose to live out their (homosexual) orientation in a partnership that is marked by faithfulness and life-giving holiness" should not be excluded from the ministry.[14] The congregation he visits might well agree. Indeed, a 1993 survey by the National and International Religion Report indicated that 75 percent of U.S. Episcopalians think sexually active gays can still be faithful Christians.[15]

Among Presbyterians he would find an ongoing debate dating back to at least 1970, when a church panel declared that "sexual expression cannot be confined to the married or about-to-be-married."[16] The panel's recommendation was narrowly voted down. The discussion continues, though the Presbyterian General Assembly in 1991 rejected a similar report that claimed a "moral right" to sexual expression for "all persons, whether heterosexual or homosexual, single or partnered."[17]

Among the United Methodist congregations, the visitor might stop by the Foundry Methodist Church in Washington DC that is home to, among others, President and Mrs. Bill Clinton. There he might hear a visiting speaker describe the apostle Paul as a "self-hating gay man," or he might listen as Foundry's pastor considers whether or not Jesus was a cross-dressing "drag queen."[18]

(Although the official Methodist position on homosexuality is far more conservative than Foundry's, unorthodox ideas about the apostle Paul and homosexuality are hardly new to Methodism. Victor Paul Furnish of Southern Methodist University, in his 1979 book, questioned whether Paul really condemned homosexuality in the New Testament.[19])

Also, when looking into the Methodist church, the visitor could choose between two diametrically opposing programs that coexist in the same denomination. Should he wish to embrace his homosexuality, he might join the Reconciling Congregations group, which advocates the pro-gay theological interpretation of Scripture. Should he decide to abandon homosexuality, the Transforming Congregations group will, thankfully, be available to him as well.

The visitor could also listen in on dialogues already underway in the Reformed Church of America to determine the appropriate view of homosexuality.[20] He could ponder the Christian Church's (Disciples of Christ) recent election of a man who favors ordination of active homo-sexuals to head their denomination.[21] And he'd be inter-ested to note that two Lutheran Churches (Evangelical Lutheran Church of America) in San Francisco recently hired homosexual ministers who refused to remain celi-bate, as ELCA church policy dictates.[22]

Surely he'd scratch his head when hearing the Rev-erend Karen Bloomquist, director of a sexuality study within the ELCA, cite "all kinds of culture wars going on around issues of sexuality in wider society" as the cause for her denomination's debate.[23]

"Culture wars in *society* dictating to *the church* what *the church* should believe?" he might well ask.

This is a frightening thought, considering cult au-thority Dr. Ron Rhodes's assessment of who should be in-fluencing whom: "The culture-forming energies of Chris-tianity depend upon the church's ability to resist the temptation to become completely identified with, or ab-sorbed into, the culture."[24]

Exactly! The very fact that we're arguing over homo-sexuality is evidence of, as radio teacher Chuck Smith says, "a sign of weakness within the church. It should not even be a question because the Bible is very clear on the subject."[25] It's also a sign of accommodation. The world's shifting morality is affecting our own, spelling a certain doom for Christianity. "When the church begins to look and sound like the world," warns Dr. Greg Bahnsen of the Southern California Center for Christian Studies, "there is no compelling rationale for its contin-ued existence."[26]

Small wonder the gay Christian movement has made such strides, considering the weakness and moral un-certainty evident in many church bodies.

By contrast, most evangelical, fundamentalist, and charismatic churches remain untouched by the debates raging in their more liberal counterparts. ("Conserva-tive" churches and denominations, in this book, are those that consistently take a traditional, literal view of the Bible; "liberal" refers to churches taking a more lenient approach to Scripture.)

Some 81 percent of conservative worshippers polled in 1991 considered homosexual acts to be wrong, and 63 percent had little patience with openly gay leadership.[27] Yet my work for the past eight years counseling Christians with sexual problems, and as a speaker to numerous Christian conferences, leads me to believe there is something amiss in conservative churches as well.

By and large, they *are* taking a clear stand against the gay philosophy, while showing indifference to, or ignorance of, the many believers in their own ranks who struggle with homosexuality. When the subject is mentioned from the pulpit, it's usually framed as a problem "out there in society" (which it is), yet few pastors add, "Perhaps someone here is wrestling with this sin, as well. Resist it—God will be with you as you do. And so will we."

As one who has known countless women and men who have renounced homosexual practices and who resist, sometimes daily, temptations to return to them, I can attest to the world of difference one remark like that from a pastor can make.

This negligence of a significant problem among believers can be found in Christian outreach or support programs, as well. Special ministries exist in many churches for people dealing with chemical dependency, alcoholism, marital problems, post-abortion trauma, emotional dependency, and eating disorders, yet the question I heard the gay minister pose 18 years ago— "Why don't they do anything to help us get over our sin?"—remains largely unanswered.

One possible reason for this is ignorance. Conservative Christians may simply be unable to believe that such a problem could be plaguing one of their own. "I've never run across that in *my* church," a local minister assured me when I tried to acquaint him with my ministry to repentant homosexuals. A sense of ethics kept me from informing him that his own choir director came to me twice a week for counseling.

Reluctance to tackle the messy issues homosexuality raises might be another reason, though there's a certain inconsistency in that. I remember a friend of mine once suggesting to a pastor that his church might develop a support group for men wanting to overcome homosexuality. "That's unnecessary," the minister retorted. "We believe in the power of the Word to transform lives. We teach people the Bible and send them home; we're not professional counselors."

No, they are not, and no one was asking them to hire any. But this same church had, weeks earlier, started a support group for people who were "co-dependent." Moreover, a group for the chemically addicted had been meeting there for years, and, sadly, one of this man's former associate ministers had fallen into homosexuality and died of AIDS.

Why the double standard? Why weren't the co-dependent, the drug addicted, and the alcoholics also just "taught the Bible and sent home"? Why the willingness, in this church and so many others, to let pastors or group leaders address such psychologically complex problems as addiction and dependency, while relegating the homosexual issue to "professional counselors"?

Of course, many fine churches have no support groups of *any* sort, and who is to say they should? But among the thousands of churches that *do* offer special care for a myriad of other problems, it seems odd that so little is offered to the repentant homosexual.

And so he finds himself between two voices (the liberal and the conservative Christian), both of whom are repeating part—but *only* part—of Christ's words to another sexual sinner, the adulterous woman: "Neither do I condemn you; go and sin no more" (John 8:11 NKJV).

"Neither do I condemn you," the liberal theologian comforts today's homosexual. "Go and sin."

"I condemn you," the conservative Christian too often retorts, and advises, "Go and sin no more!"—and then leaves the sinner alone to figure out how.

Or else he just says, "Go!"

Naturally the gay Christian movement looks so appealing to the woman or man struggling with homosexuality. It offers them acceptance and understanding that they may never have found in the church.

That does not absolve them of responsibility if, like me, they decide to embrace pro-gay theology. But if we have offered them little help on their way toward making that decision, don't we bear some responsibility, too?

Ron Rhodes makes a good observation on this point:

> A person does not usually join a cult because he has done an exhaustive analysis of world religions and has decided that a particular cult presents the best theology available. Instead, a person generally joins a cult because he has problems that he is having trouble solving, and the cult promises to solve these problems.[28]

But *we* can promise to solve the problems, too. We can begin by confronting the expanding gay Christian movement, refuting its erroneous claims, and equipping ourselves to answer its revisions of the Bible. We can learn to intelligently debate pro-gay advocates in our denominations by knowing their arguments and the reasoning behind them.

We can promise to develop a more effective response to the repentant homosexuals in our churches who crave—*and deserve*—our support. Having done that, we can address the broader gay rights movement, by faithfully stewarding truth and love, refusing to compromise one for the sake of the other.

Promises such as these are long overdue, but many believers today seem eager to both make and keep them. That's why this book—*A Strong Delusion*—was written.

Since 1991 I have presented a series of talks titled "Answering the Pro-Gay Theology" at conferences and seminars. Several people have mentioned how helpful the series would be if put into written form. Members of denominations that are debating the issue said it could be a valuable tool. And family members have said it could help them better understand their sons, daughters, or siblings who are part of the gay Christian movement.

I have also noticed how few Christians are aware that there is such a thing as pro-gay theology, much less a movement built around it. And many who are aware of it have no idea how to answer its claims. This book was written for them, as well.

Four things seem necessary to effectively confront the gay Christian movement:

1. An understanding of the evolution and nature of the movement.

2. A point-by-point knowledge of its beliefs.

3. A point-by-point response to each belief.

4. A practical plan of action the church can take in response to the gay Christian movement.

With that in mind, the first four chapters of this book will overview the importance of the subject and provide some background on the gay Christian movement and the influences in modern Christianity that have contributed to it.

Chapters 6 through 9 will detail the main arguments of the pro-gay theology, breaking them into three basic groups, and providing a specific answer to each. A sample dialogue/debate will be provided at the end of each of these chapters as a model for future discussions the reader may have. I've been especially eager to write these sample dialogues because of the number of times I hear questions such as:

• "What do you say to a homosexual who says he's born that way?"

• "How do you answer gays or lesbians who say they're Christians and that they believe the Bible, too?"

• "Leaders in my denomination think we should start ordaining openly homosexual ministers. How can we stand against this?"

These, and several other similar questions, are posed and answered in chapters 7 through 9. I trust that they will prove useful in whatever future dialogues the reader may have on this subject.

Chapter 11 will offer an action plan by which readers can respond to the gay Christian movement, whether it involves someone they love or a debate over homosexuality within their denomination. The final chapter will offer some personal concluding thoughts on this important issue.

"Sanctify the Lord God in your hearts," Peter admonished. "And be ready always to give an answer to every man that asketh you a reason of the hope that is in you, with meekness and fear" (1 Peter 3:15).

This book was written toward that end, and with the hope that it will equip the servant of the Lord, as Paul so aptly said, to:

> not strive, but be gentle unto all men, apt to teach, patient,
>
> In meekness instructing those who oppose themselves;
>
> If God peradventure will give them repentance to the acknowledging of the truth;
>
> And that they may recover themselves out of the snare of the devil, who are taken captive by him at his will.
>
> (2 Timothy 2:24–26)

As one who was graciously given repentance to the acknowledging of the truth, I hope that *A Strong Delusion* will be useful to those who can instruct, and to those needing instruction.

They are both everywhere.

1

Why Bother?

*"The church must be reminded that it is not
the master or servant of the state, but rather
the conscience of the state."*

— Martin Luther King

few years ago I was interviewed by a radio
host who couldn't understand my concern over homosexuality. "Why do you
bother with this subject?" he asked. "Why the big fuss
over homosexuality in the church?"

"Because it's more of a problem than most Christians realize," I answered. "Some of us are ignoring it,
and others are butchering the Bible to accommodate it."

"So?" he pressed. "Would it really kill you to bend a
little? If all the churches in America could relax and see
that homosexuality is just another way people love each
other, would that be so awful? Exactly what horrible
thing would happen?"

That flabbergasted me. "Are you kidding? It would be
a disaster!" I fumed. "It would confuse everyone, it would
disregard the Bible, it would—it would—"

I was still sputtering when he broke for a commercial.

Actually, he had posed an important question, and I
responded with knee-jerk emotion instead of clear answers. I've heard other Christians make the same mistake

27

when speaking on this subject. We tend to be better at showing how strongly we object to homosexuality than we are at explaining *why* we object so strongly.

So what exactly is it we're so worried about? Is resisting the gay Christian movement worth the time and energy it will inevitably take? *Why bother?*

There are plenty of answers one could offer, I'm sure, but let me cite the ones that have influenced my approach over the years. I believe there are five general, drastic consequences we will face if we fail to confront the gay Christian movement, all of which have begun to emerge even now, but are, to a large degree, restrained by the church's influence. The first two are spiritual consequences, and will be discussed in this chapter:

1. A denigration of the authority of the Bible.

2. The fruit of misrepresentation and disobedience.

3. The sexual exploitation of children.

The next three are cultural, and will be discussed in chapter two:

4. Increased sexual confusion among the young.

5. A further, but significant, loss of family definition.

Whether or not we have to face these consequences will largely be determined by the success of the gay Christian movement.

It is a given that, if not confronted, the movement will succeed. A friend of mine, who ministers in a denomination that's now wrestling with the issue, says that some of his fellow conservative pastors don't want to argue over it: "They think that liberal pastors who take a pro-gay position will eventually resign or give up, so there's no need to worry."

But that is wishful thinking. A quick glance at the determination that pro-gay groups have shown when pursuing their goals in the Presbyterian, United Metho-dist, Episcopal, and Disciples of Christ churches—not to mention the Metropolitan Community Church's decade-long effort to be recognized by the World Council of Churches proves that the gay Christian movement is nothing if not tenacious.[1]

If the church is unable to resist this movement, it will result in a change of standards in most mainline Protestant denominations—and quite possibly many independent, fundamentalist, evangelical, and charismatic churches. Thus America may one day receive, *from her own churches*, a definition of family standards that includes (and approves of) gay marriage, civil protection for homosexual acts, education (beginning with the primary grades) on the normality of homosexuality, and the general portrayal of same-sex unions as healthy and legitimate.

Not all churches will go along with this, certainly, but no matter; if the majority or even a significant percentage of them cave-in to gay ideology, it will amount to a religious sanctioning of the gay movement's demands. No one knows this better than gay leadership. Gay columnist Paul Varnell states:

> The chief opposition to gay equality is religious. We may conduct much of our liberation efforts in the political sphere or even the "cultural" sphere, but always undergirding those and slowing our progress is the moral/religious sphere. If we could hasten the pace of change there, our overall progress would accelerate—in fact, it would be assured.[2]

With that assurance, normality and morality will have been successfully redefined, and both church and society will begin to reap the spiritual and cultural consequences.

The Denigration of Biblical Authority

The body of Christ will suffer immeasurably because sound doctrine—and even the Bible itself—will *have* to be taken less seriously if the pro-gay theology is widely accepted. You simply cannot tamper with one part of

Scripture (in this case, a very significant part) without dismantling its authority in general. And when the authority of the Bible is denigrated, the church of Jesus Christ, the light of the world, will be without any clear guidance of her own.

When I belonged to the Metropolitan Community Church (MCC) I saw this dilemma firsthand. At that time, there was an ongoing debate between their conservative and liberal congregations. Many leaders and members of the MCC were from fundamentalist/evangelical backgrounds, and continued to refer to themselves as theologically conservative. (Their "Statement of Faith," in fact, contains the basics most Christians agree on.) But others held radical, sometimes blasphemous views.

One minister wrote in the MCC's official publication that it was idolatry to worship Jesus as God. Another stated in print her discomfort with the cross, implying a link between references to the blood of Christ and sadomasochism. And on at least one occasion I spoke with a pastor who said he wasn't sure what being born again meant, so he had no intention of encouraging people to do it.[3]

When conservatives in the MCC argued for a return to biblical authority, their liberal opponents reminded them that the position they *all* shared on homosexuality was at odds with Christian tradition and conservatism, so how could they (the conservatives) now push for biblical literalism? That was an argument I never heard a convincing rebuttal to.

"The Bible," Hank Hanegraaff of the Christian Research Institute states, "not only forms the foundation of an effective prayer life, but it is fundamental to every other aspect of Christian living—[it] is God's primary way of communicating with us."[4] When God's primary way of communicating with us is compromised, an ancient sin is revived in which compromised obedience to God in *one* area cripples respect for His Word in other, *perhaps* all, areas of life and conduct.

It began when Eve allowed herself to mull over the serpent's question, "Hath God said?" (Genesis 3:1). Notice that Eve did not reject God's instructions entirely; she simply listened as the serpent explained their "unfairness." The satanic argument, as always, was couched in the most reasonable of terms—"Is it really *fair* for God to not want you to be like Him?" (see Genesis 3:4–5).

Eve bought the "unfairness" argument and it's an argument people are *still* buying.

"It is inconceivable to me that God would create someone like me who is unable to change," a lesbian minister asserts, and "then condemn that person to hell."[5]

A familiar theme: God's standards seem unfair; therefore, they must not really be God's standards. No matter how sincerely gay Christians claim to believe in biblical authority, their compromise in this one area weakens their position in others as well.

It will weaken the church's position on issues of life and conduct, too. Before accepting the pro-gay theological view, we might consider the diminished respect for biblical authority and lowering of standards in other areas that are evident in the gay Christian movement.

Gay author and minister Mel White (formerly of Fuller Theological Seminary), for example, describes his first homosexual encounter (which he engaged in while he was still married) as "inevitable." He describes his partner in adultery/homosexuality as "one of God's gifts."[6]

Troy Perry, a former pastor with the Church of God and the founder of the Metropolitan Community Church, takes a similar view of a similar experience. Recounting a tryst he had with another man (while his own wife was in the next room), he recalls: "Eventually, I came to realize that what we were doing seemed right for me. It stopped short of being love, but was a marvelous education."[7]

Adultery described as "right" and as "a marvelous education"? Does acceptance of homosexuality lead to an altered view of marital commitment in general? It certainly did for Perry, who stated in a 1989 interview that adultery involves the breaking of vows made to another person, which may not necessarily be vows of fidelity: "If you have an open [inclusive of other sexual partners] relationship, that's fine and dandy."[8]

It is unlikely that Reverend Perry taught such loose views of marriage when he served as a pastor with the Church of God. Reverend White, likewise, could hardly have written of an adulterous encounter as "inevitable," nor of a companion in either homosexual or heterosexual adultery as "God's gift," when he was a professor of preaching and communications at Fuller Theological Seminary. Something changed in their understanding of fidelity; the change cannot be unrelated to their acceptance of the gay theology.

The first openly gay Episcopal priest to be ordained, Robert Williams, goes further than Perry and White by declaring in *Newsweek* magazine, on the subject of monogamy: "If people want to try, OK. But the fact is, people are not monogamous. It is crazy to hold up this ideal and pretend it's what we're doing, and we're not."[9] Williams ends his remarks with an unusually tasteless flourish when he suggests, in the most vulgar terms, that Mother Theresa ought to have a sexual experience.[10]

The late Reverend Sylvia Pennington, a heterosexual advocate for the gay Christian movement, included an alleged revelation about marriage and divorce in her book-long argument against the possibility of anyone overcoming homosexuality:

> When any human relationship begins to infringe on the most important and eternal relationship—which is our union with Christ—the Lord Himself will end that human relationship. When the pain of an unsuccessful marriage begins to separate either party from God, then it is God, and not the people, who ends the marriage.[11]

Contrary to Jesus' specific reference to fornication as being the only grounds for divorce (Matthew 19:9), Reverend Pennington gave the go-ahead, to anyone feeling that his or her marriage has begun to "infringe" on his or her relationship with God, for divorce proceedings.

The Presbyterian Task Force, in their gay-affirming 1991 report titled "Keeping Body and Soul Together," didn't even bother with inconvenient concepts such as marriage and monogamy. Instead they opted for the clever notion of "Justice Love," declaring that appropriate sexual conduct should be judged by "whether the relationship is responsible, the dynamics genuinely mutual, and the loving full of joyful caring."[12] One need not dwell too long on the carnal varieties and combinations one could call "responsible, mutual, and full of joyful caring."

Can such low moral standards among people naming the name of Christ reflect anything but a diminished view of Scripture? While most in the gay Christian movement insist that they consider the Bible to be authoritative, a look at some of their remarks about Scripture betrays another view:

> What influences lead us to new ways of understanding Scripture? *New scientific information, social change, and personal experience* are perhaps the greatest forces for change in the way we interpret the Bible and develop our beliefs (emphasis added).
>
> —Troy Perry[13]

> [In reference to the apostle Paul's views on homosexuality.] "So what? Paul was wrong about any number of other things, too. Why should you take him any more seriously than you take Jerry Falwell, Anita Bryant, or Cardinal O' Connor?
>
> —Robert Williams[14]

> I can no longer worship in a theological context that depicts God as an abusive parent and Je-

sus as the obedient, trusting child. This violent
theology encourages the violence in our streets
and nations.

—Lesbian author Virginia Mollenkott[15]

Jane Spahr, cofounder of CLOUT (Christian
Lesbians Out Together) and lesbian evangelist
for the Downtown Presbyterian Church of
Rochester, claimed her theology was first of all
informed by "making love with Coni," her lesbian partner.[16]

I know in my heart that the canon is not
closed—I know this because the Bible does not
reconcile me with the earth and the Bible does
not reconcile me with my sexual self.

—Melanie Morrison, cofounder of CLOUT[17]

Again, it should be understood that many in the gay
Christian movement would disagree with some of the
above remarks. Some would even find them outrageous.
But compromise begets compromise; the disrespect for
biblical standards among the radical elements of the gay
Christian movement is the unquestionable result of the
biblical revisions the movement itself is based on.

Can we expect any less to happen in our own sanctuaries if we, as the gay Christian movement did, allow
a similar compromise to biblical integrity?

The Fruit of Misrepresentation and Disobedience

The church will surely incur God's displeasure if His
Word is compromised or misrepresented. And as a result, our influence and effectiveness in this world will be
weakened, if not erased.

When David and his armies brought the ark of God
from Judah to Jerusalem, they had been given specific
instructions by God regarding its maintenance and
transportation (1 Samuel 6:1-8). One rule was clear:

after it was prepared for travel, the ark—a "holy thing"—
was not to be touched (Numbers 4:15). But during the
trip to Jerusalem the cart that was transporting the ark
began to shake, and one of the drivers (Uzzah) with the
best of intentions grabbed the ark to steady it.

He was struck dead on the spot (2 Samuel 6:7).
God's instructions had been clear; His holiness was not
to be compromised or misrepresented by an unautho-
rized touch.

Misrepresentation and disobedience were also Moses'
downfall. God had told him, when the Israelites were
thirsting in the desert of Zin, to speak to the rock in front
of him, and water would come out of it to quench their
thirst (Numbers 20:1-8).

But Moses was fed up with the people's complaints.
So, in a fit of temper, he struck the rock twice instead of
speaking to it. Like Uzzah, he paid with his life for disobedience (Numbers 27:12-14) and for misrepresenting God
to His people. (The rock, according to 1 Corinthians 10:4,
symbolized Christ, who was smitten once and for all—not
twice—for the sins of the world.) God would not tolerate a
misrepresentation of such an important concept.

How, then, must God view religious leaders who condone misrepresentation of one of the most important
concepts revealed in Scripture: that of God's love for His
people, typified in the union of husband and wife?

In both the Old and New Testaments, marriage is used
to illustrate and represent God and Israel, as well as Christ
and the church (Isaiah 54:5; Jeremiah 31:32; Ezekiel
16:21-32; Hosea 2:19; Ephesians 5:25; Revelation 21:2).
The marriage model is complimentary—*male to female*—
with no hint of sexual sameness between the parties.

*What displeasure will we incur if we sanction a clear
misrepresentation of God and His beloved?*

When such precise and easily understood instructions have been given in Scripture regarding the nature of
marriage, what will the church suffer if she, with good
intentions like Uzzah's or with a carelessness like Moses',

misrepresents and disobeys God by distorting His intentions for sexual love?

And won't the church's life, like Uzzah's, be drained away, leaving her unable to influence the culture around her? Can she, in that condition, lead people into the promised land, or will she, like Moses, be stopped short, never able to enter in?

God is not mocked. No matter how loudly we sacrifice our praise in our modern churches, if we've done it while condoning a perversion of God's intent for the most basic of human relations, we will be reminded that to obey is better than sacrifice. I shudder to think how that reminder might come.

2

Cultural Consequences

"This is why lines must be drawn, standards discussed, and battles fought. Because when people push the envelope of morality and get away with it, they don't sit back to enjoy the sensation. They reach further—touching the lives of the people around them—touching the lives of your children, and someday, mine.."

— Kristi Hamrick, press secretary,
Family Research Council

T he next three consequences of ignoring the gay Christian movement are more cultural than spiritual, having long-range implications for the next generation.

Jesus called us the salt of the earth and said that if we (as salt) lose our savor, we will be impotent in our impact on the world (Matthew 5:13). Paul likewise viewed the church as a restraining influence, whose very presence in the world hindered evil forces (2 Thessalonians 2:7). When our influence is weakened through compromise, our ability to restrain evil in the world is nullified, and our culture suffers the consequences.

The organized body of Christ represents virtually the last voice raised in protest against the gay rights movement.[1] If that voice is silenced, or its message compromised, the gay Christian movement will anoint the gay rights movement to steamroll the country. And the next generation will be the first to feel the brunt of it.

The Sexual Exploitation of Children

At the outset, let me clarify that I do not view homosexuality and pedophilia (sex between adults and children) as the same. While both are clearly immoral and unnatural, they also involve different behaviors, cross different moral boundaries, and evoke different consequences.

Likewise, I do not assume that homosexual men are likely—*simply because they're homosexual*—to molest children.[2] As a survivor of sexual abuse, I take the issue seriously and am open to any data on the subject. But what I have observed firsthand (which is limited, certainly) leads me to believe that most homosexuals are not interested in sexual relations with children.

I have counseled more than 100 homosexual men and a handful (five or less) of pedophiles.[3] None of the men who identified themselves as homosexuals reported any sexual feelings whatsoever for children. Of the pedophiles I counseled, none reported being aroused by adult men of the same sex, furthering my belief that homosexuality and pedophilia ought to be viewed as separate conditions.

My experiences in the gay community also confirmed this. As a staff member, delegate, and pianist of the Metropolitan Community Church, I knew hundreds of gay men. Not one of them, to my knowledge, had any sexual interest in children.

Still, I am convinced that the acceptance of homosexuality will pave the way for the acceptance of pedophilia. This is so, not because homosexuals necessarily desire sex with children, but because the approval of one previously taboo practice makes room for the next, more serious taboo.

In the early 1960s, before the "Sexual Revolution" hit, the two major taboos were adultery and fornication. Both were generally frowned on, and those who practiced them usually kept quiet about it. Then, during the upheaval characterizing the 60s, people began to take a kinder and gentler view of these practices. Films such as *The Graduate*, *Love Story*, and *Bob and Carol and Ted and Alice* began portraying these practices in first a sympathetic, then downright positive light. Popular songs like "Let's Spend the Night Together" glamorized them; theater productions such as *Hair* and *Oh! Calcutta!* portrayed them on stage and comedians joked about them.

Soon what was taboo became commonplace. And homosexuality began peeking out from behind the next curtain.

By and large, those who broke the taboos in the 60s didn't openly support homosexuality. It was seldom mentioned, much less promoted, and when it was discussed it was done in less than sympathetic terms. (Even the hippie movement, with its Woodstock excesses of nudity and public sex, had no room for homosexuality.) Yet the swingers of the 60s were the unwilling doormen for the budding gay rights movement. If sex between consenting men and women apart from marriage was now permissible, after all, then why not between consenting adults of the same sex?

The marriage boundary around sexual behavior had been removed. The next boundary's removal was less than five years away.

Films toward the end of the 60s and the early to mid 1970s—*Boys in the Band*, *Fortune in Men's Eyes*, *Norman Is That You?*—portrayed homosexuality in first a sympathetic, and then positive light. Popular songs such as "Lola" glamorized it. Theater productions like *The Ritz* and *Fortune in Men's Eyes* portrayed it on stage. And, comedians again, joked about it. Homosexuality's biggest boost toward acceptance came when the American Psychiatric Association removed homosexuality from its list of disorders. Supporters of this decision argued that:

1. *Homosexuality represented a problem only to those homosexuals who were distressed by it.* "If a homosexual is distressed about his orientation, the appropriate diagnosis should be the underlying psychological disorder, e.g. anxiety reaction—depressive reaction" (Dr. Judd Marmor in recommendations to the American Psychiatric Association).[4]

2. *Society's antihomosexual prejudice had created more problems for homosexuals than their sexuality had.* "We are told, from the time we first recognize our homosexual feelings, that our love . . . is sick . . . that we are emotional cripples. . . . The result of this in many cases is to contribute to a self-image that often lowers the sights we set for ourselves in life" (memo from gay organizations in New York City to the American Psychiatric Association).[5]

3. *Homosexuals were no less emotionally stable than heterosexuals.* The Chair of the APA Task Force "concluded that homosexuals showed no significant signs of pathology."[23]

4. *Homosexual relationships could be healthy and affirming.* The Chair of the APA Task Force "concluded that a significant portion of homosexuals . . . could function well interpersonally."[7]

The arguments worked. The Board of the American Psychiatric Association voted to change the diagnostic status of homosexuality. (See chapter 7 for a full account of the events leading up to the APA vote.)

This landmark decision began with a group of gays who gathered data, networked, and rallied support from a culture that was reluctant (at first) to accept them, and they effectively utilized their allies within the leadership of the American Psychiatric Association.[8] Pedophilia watched from behind the next curtain, waiting.

Today, we are hearing the same arguments from "experts" defending pedophilia as we heard 20 years ago from those defending homosexuality:

1. *Pedophilia represents a problem only to those pedophiles who are distressed by it.* "According to the new DSM-IV (*Diagnostic and Statistical Manual of the American Psychiatric Association*) a pedophile [has a diagnosable condition] ONLY if he feels bad or anxious about what he's doing" (newsletter from the National Association of Research and Treatment of Homosexuality on recent diagnostic reclassifications).[9]

2. *Society's antipedophile prejudice creates more problems for pedophiles than their sexuality does.* William Pomeroy, formerly of the Alfred Kinsey Research Team, "told *Citizen* magazine that adult-child sex can be 'wonderful and beautiful,' adding that the only downside is that the 'consequences' society applies against such behavior 'can be absolutely horrendous'" (interview of sex researcher Pomeroy in Focus on the Family's *Citizen* magazine).[10]

3. *Pedophiles are no less emotionally stable than nonpedophiles.* "Pedophilia, according to [Dr. John] Money, should be viewed as a sexual orientation, not a disease or a disorder."[11]

4. *Child-adult relationships can be healthy and affirming.* "People seem to think that any contact between children and adults . . . has a bad effect on the child. I say this can be a loving and thoughtful, responsible sexual activity."[12]

Culture has been lagging behind the "experts" on this subject. No songs or plays have yet, to my knowledge, lauded pedophilia, and I've heard no stand-up routines on the subject.

However, a recent independent film, praised by the *New York Times* as "a delicate story of aching tenderness."[13] portrayed the sexual relationship between a 13-year-old boy and an adult soldier in a romantic, positive way. (A photo of the two lying together was even displayed in print ads.) This film, *For a Lost Soldier*, was not a major hit. Few people saw it; it came and went with little fanfare. But I doubt it will be the last of its kind.

Meanwhile, as gay activists before them did, advocates of pedophilia are gathering data, networking, and rallying support from a culture reluctant to accept them, and they are utilizing their allies within the leadership of the American Psychiatric Association. Those allies already include:

• Dr. John Money of Johns Hopkins University, who, in an interview with *The Journal of Pedophilia* in the Netherlands, said: "If I were to see a case of a boy aged 10 or 11 who's intensely erotically attracted toward a man in his twenties or thirties, if the relationship is mutual—then I would not call it pathological in any way."[14]

• Dr. Deryck Calderwood, chairman of the SIECUS (Sex Information and Education Council of the US) Board of Directors, who said: "When no one gives the child a bad conscience . . . intercourse between adults and children causes no mental harm."[15]

• Dr. John DeCecco, professor and head of the Human Sexuality Department at San Francisco State University, who said: "The decision [to have child/adult sex] should largely rest in the hands of the people who are entering into the relationship. If I'm 12 and I decide to have sex with a 19-year-old or a 20-year-old or a 50-year-old, that is really a choice I have."[16]

• Dr. Wayne Dynes, professor at Hunter College, who shares DeCecco's views: "[I'm] not sure that a 7-year-old can give informed consent. That doesn't mean that one should necessarily exclude sexual relations with them."[17]

• Lester Kirkendall, Ph.D., SIECUS founding board member, who anticipates that future sex education programs "will probe sexual expression . . . across generational lines. These patterns will become legitimate."[18]

• Harvard Health Services psychologist Douglas Powell, who said: "I have not seen anyone harmed by this [child-adult sex] so long as it occurs in a relationship with somebody who really cares about the child."[19]

But even with blessings from the academic elite, could the advocates of pedophilia really win the public's sympathy, much less its approval? Unthinkable.

But then, public approval of homosexuality was unthinkable 30 years ago. We should know by now that a campaign's success depends not on its rightness, but on how well it's packaged and how aggressively it is promoted. In this respect, Dr. Money advises pedophiles to take their cue from gay activists:

> When the gay rights activists became politically active, there wasn't a sufficient body of scientific information for them to base their gay activism on. So, you don't have to have a basic body of scientific information in order to decide to work actively for a particular ideology. As long as you're prepared to be put in jail. Isn't that how social change has always taken place, really?[20]

In an interview on the "700 Club" three years ago, I cited many of these quotes as evidence that the gay rights movement was serving as a doorman to the pedophile movement. Is this really what gays want?

I doubt it. Leadership in the gay community is divided over what support, if any, it should lend the pedophile movement. NAMBLA (the North American Man-Boy Love Association, founded in 1977, and the most visible pedophile organization) petitioned to march in the Stonewall 25 Gay Pride Parade. They had the support of *some* gay leaders, yet the organizers of the parade banned them from participating.[21]

Some gays openly denounce both NAMBLA and any form of adult-child sex. Others see NAMBLA as a logical extension of the gay community.[22] One thing is certain, though: the pedophile movement could not have made any significant gains if the gay rights movement hadn't paved the way by challenging existing norms and restrictions on sexual behavior.

This brings us back to the church. If the church—unable or unwilling to confront the gay Christian movement—yields to it, the gay Christian movement will, with religious authority, open the door for the gay rights movement to overhaul America's values. And, whether deliberately or not, the gay rights movement will then hold the door for the pedophile movement and its own pernicious agenda.

History will hopefully run its course before we see what's biding its time behind the *next* curtain.[23]

Increased Sexual Confusion Among the Young

A photocopy of a very enlightening letter appears in Dr. James Dobson's book, *Children at Risk*:

> American Civil Liberties Union
> California Legislative Branch
> 1127 11th Street Suite 605
> Sacramento, California 95814
>
> May 26, 1988
>
> Members, Assembly Education Committee
> State Capitol
> Sacramento, CA 95814
>
> Dear Members:
>   The ACLU regrets to inform you of our opposition to SB 2394 concerning sex education in public schools.
>   It is our position that teaching monogamous, heterosexual intercourse within marriage is a traditional American value is an unconstitutional establishment of a religious doctrine in public schools. There are various religions that hold contrary beliefs with respect to marriage

and monogamy. We believe SB 2394 violates the First Amendment.

Very truly yours,

Marjorie C. Swartz
Executive Director[24]

In response to offensive sex education programs, several California conservatives—many of them Christian—pushed for the passage of SB 2394. The bill called for recognition, in the public school system, of heterosexual intercourse within marriage as being a traditional American value, and mandated the teaching of abstinence in sex education.[25]

The American Civil Liberty Union's response is noteworthy in that it typifies the resistance we can expect when we confront the moral deterioration in our schools. (It should be noted that, while objecting to ideals as radical as "abstinence" and "monogamy," the ACLU seems to have no problem approving the sale and distribution of child pornography.[26])

The legislation passed and is in place today. But what if the Christian voice on morality had been neutralized? What if the church had, by 1988, largely accepted the gay Christian movement's beliefs? Would Christians in churches promoting homosexuality have considered pushing for legislation to promote heterosexuality within marriage? Not likely.

If most denominations had caved-in to the movement, and it was common knowledge that most churches taught the legitimacy of homosexuality, would those few Christians who pushed for this legislation have any credibility before the California Assembly? Or would they look like a minority of fringe-group extremists, wholly out of touch with modern Christianity and unable to stand up to the ACLU?

More to the point: If the gay Christian movement succeeds, what influences will shape our children's ideas about sexuality? To get a clear picture, one need only look at efforts being made now, even with a clear Christian opposition, to indoctrinate the next generation into a pro-gay ideology.

Project 10, a counseling program founded by lesbian teacher Virginia Uribe, bills itself as "a dropout prevention program" offering support and information to students "who identify themselves as lesbian, gay, or bisexual, or who want accurate information about sexual orientation."[27] Its title comes from the universally discredited notion that ten percent of the population is homosexual, a notion still promoted to students in programs like this one. (See chapter 6 for a discussion of Kinsey's ten percent statistic.)

A book distributed by Project 10, *One Teenager in 10: Writings About Gay and Lesbian Youth*, features first-person testimonials by lesbian and gay teenagers on their "coming out process" and related issues. In the original version of the book (which was distributed to students before it was revised), a testimonial by a 16-year-old girl named Amy details, in graphic terms worthy of a pornographic novel, her first sexual encounter at age 12 with her 23-year-old female dance instructor (culminating in a three-year affair). The illegality, not to mention the immorality, of a 23-year-old teacher having sex with a 13-year-old girl is not addressed in the book; it simply presents the story as one of many positive "awakenings."[28]

When made aware of the contents of *One Teenager in 10*, outraged parents in Southern California protested to their school board, and the offensive chapter has since been removed. But the fact remains that, in its original form, *One Teenager in 10*—with its glowing description of the molestation of a 13-year-old girl—had the support of the Project 10 counseling program.

A worse scenario appeared on the East Coast in the early 90s. In the New York City public school system, sex education materials distributed to students taught them about their right to have sex with whomever they want, the sexiness of condoms, the pleasures of oral sex and masturbation, the use of sex toys, and assorted practices involving urine and feces.[29]

When the New York City Queens (District 24) School Board members voted to reject a curriculum guide that advised first-grade teachers to "include reference to lesbians/gay people in all curricular areas" (no matter what subject is being taught a reference to homosexuality was suggested), they were demonstrated against, "pilloried" by the press, and suspended from their duties by the school chancellor![30]

Outraged parents, again, forced their reinstatement and voiced their disapproval of the pro-gay curriculum.

In an unusual turn of events, the openly lesbian president of the Gay and Lesbian Resource Center in Ojai, California, has accused gay activists of "using federal AIDS-education money to . . . conduct explicit educational programs in public schools, and recruit children into the homosexual lifestyle." Children in public schools, she said, "are encouraged to experiment sexually."[31]

If these conditions exist when organized protest from the church *is present*, what might our children face in the *absence* of such resistance?

Lesbian teacher Virginia Uribe's ambitious plan gives us a clue: "The State Courts must be used to force the school districts to disseminate accurate information about homosexuality. Starting in the kindergarten, again, and working its way all the way through high school. This is war."[32] Considering the title of her program—"Project 10," based on "accurate information" that's been repeatedly disproven —one wonders what other "accuracies" she hopes the courts will foist on students.

Sponsors of programs such as Dr. Uribe's seek to assure us that they "don't recruit, because homosexuality is not a choice."[33] So we can relax, they say special instruction on homosexuality and sex education will not confuse our kids about their own sexual identity.

Oh really? Being reminded about sexual variations, beginning in first grade, in *every* subject ("It's math time, children! Now, if two lesbians are artificially inseminated by one bisexual doctor, how many gay sons will they be statistically inclined to have?"), being taught about condom usage, masturbation, the right to indiscriminate sex, how to use sex toys, being instructed in the art of sharing body waste-materials while being reminded that ten percent of their classmates are gay or lesbian *and* being recruited to experiment homosexually to such an extent that even the president of a Gay and Lesbian Resource Center complains—*this will not leave them confused about their sexual identity?*

By the time a student runs the erotic gauntlet waiting for him in some public schools, how can he not be affected? The fact is, confusion about sexual identity during adolescence is common under the best of circumstances, and teenagers shouldn't be exploited with premature suggestions about what their sexual identity is or isn't.

This was verified in the Minnesota Adolescent Health Survey of 1992, which surveyed 34,706 students in Minnesota secondary schools. The subjects were questioned about their sexual orientation—whether they were heterosexual, homosexual, or unsure. The results showed how common it is for uncertainty about one's sexuality in early adolescence to resolve itself by the later teens: 25.9 percent of the 12-year-olds were unsure whether they were heterosexual or homosexual, whereas only five percent of the 17-year-olds surveyed were similarly unsure. (Some 98.5 percent of all the students reported being sure they were heterosexual.)[34] In other words, children between the age of 12 and 17 are often uncertain about their sexual preferences.

The New Kinsey Report on sex indicated the same when responding to a teenager's question about homosexual feelings: "It's not uncommon for people your age to feel confused about their sexual feelings. It's important to remember that sexual feelings aroused by a person of the same sex . . . are not accurate predictors of your adult sexual orientation."[35]

If it's not uncommon for young adolescents to feel confused about their sexual identity—unsure whether they're homosexual or heterosexual—and if they're being encouraged during those same confusing years to experiment sexually, and if they're taught that virtually all forms of sexual expression are legitimate, then when parents are told, "Don't worry, we don't recruit; if your kid is not gay, these programs can't make him gay," can they really be expected to buy it?

E. L. Pattullo, the former director for the Center of Behavioral Sciences at Harvard University, does not think so:

> It's a good bet that substantial numbers of children have the capacity to grow in either [a homosexual or heterosexual] direction. Such young waverers, who until now have been raised in an environment overwhelmingly biased toward heterosexuality, might succumb to the temptations of homosexuality in a social climate that was entirely evenhanded in its treatment of the two orientations.[36]

Interestingly enough, Donna Minkowitz, a well-known lesbian columnist, shares Dr. Pattullo's belief that recruitment is possible, while sharing none of his concern about the results:

> I'm much more comfortable with the notion of "recruiting" than I am with the guesstimate that restricts same-sex passion to a fixed percentage of the population. . . . In a world without the heterosexual imperative, maybe kids would try on different forms of sexuality as they now try on musical styles, career choices, and haircuts.[37]

If so, then children well on their way to growing up heterosexual might—according to sources as varied as the Minnesota study, the Kinsey Institute, a former Harvard behavioral science director, and a lesbian columnist—become homosexual when they had the chance for a *heterosexual* orientation and a *completely different future!*

And what of the students who would develop homosexually anyway? Is it so important for them to know, at such an early age, the sexual variations available to them? Need they be confirmed in a gay identity so early? Will the "accurate" information that Dr. Uribe is so anxious for them to have include works by experts like Sigmund Freud, Irvine Bieber, Gerard van den Aardweg, Charles Socarides, and Dr. Joseph Nicolosi, showing them that they may choose other options than a gay identity?

Don't count on it.

When they *do* opt for homosexuality, their chances of dying, indelicate though it may be to say so, are greatly increased. AIDS is still decimating the homosexual community. More frightening still, a 1991 study showed that 31 percent of the gay subjects had engaged in unprotected (without a condom) anal intercourse—one of the most unsafe sexual practices a person could choose—in the previous two months.[38] Researchers funded by the National Institute of Health estimate that, at current rates of infection, a *majority* of 20-year-old gay or bisexual men nationwide will one day have the AIDS virus.[39]

Worse yet, data in a Los Angeles, California study indicated that 50 percent of the gay 15 to 22-year-olds surveyed had recently engaged in high risk sex, and ten percent of them were already infected with the AIDS virus.[40]

Results of a more recent survey are just as bleak. In February 1996, the National Cancer Institute reported that gay men between the ages of 18 and 25 show the highest rate of HIV infection, despite the fact that they came of age long after "safe sex" campaigns were established.[41]

All of this occurs even as the church, by and large, still offers a resistance to gay counseling and sex education programs. But what if, someday, the church, having adopted a pro-gay position, stops offering this resistance?

Without resistance, these programs will educate students on the normality of homosexuality from the day they toddle into their first class. By the time a boy reaches his early teens, he will already know more than most adults currently do about sexual practices, having learned a catalogue of them from childhood on. Confused about feelings he may have for the same sex, and encouraged to explore his sexuality even if he's unsure what his preference really is, he may find himself in the arms of a 20, 30, or 50-year-old man—both man and boy having been assured by prominent psychologists that such a relationship can be "beautiful." Or, should he stick to his peers for sexual alliances, his chances of HIV infection, unless the practices and rates of infection change among teenagers and young adults, will be high.

Having begun life with a good shot at marriage and family, he may end it in his twenties on a respirator, emaciated and terrified, but with an education on sexuality from grades 1 to 12 that he can take to the grave.

The Loss of Family Definition

Of the three cultural consequences I believe we will suffer—the other two being the sexual exploitation of children and sexual confusion among the young—the loss of family definition will be both the reason for, and the result of, the other two.

If the church allows marriage to be redefined to include same-sex couples, then a circular deterioration will start: there will be an increase in the sexual confusion and exploitation of children as a result of the redefinition of family, and there will be an even further redefinition of family as a result of the sexual confusion and exploitation of children. Given enough time, the original concept of "family" could be driven right out of our consciousness.

Not that the family isn't already hurting; it is in danger, and it's *not* homosexuals who put it there. Spousal assaults, abandonment, divorce, adultery, child abuse, and incest have battered the family for years. I was once asked by a Christian radio host what I felt the greatest threat to the nuclear family was. Since the show was on homosexuality, I knew the answer she was looking for, but I couldn't give it: "The greatest threat to the nuclear family," I said sadly, "is the nuclear family."

But the family remains (as of this writing in April 1996) with its definition intact, which is crucial. So long as the family is recognized for what it *is*, and remains sanctioned as such, it can survive; its problems can be corrected. Redefine it, though, and through redefinition, it loses its very worth.

I have heard gay couples argue that they can do a fine job of raising children. Some say they are better at it than some heterosexual couples they've known.

Likewise, in the 1993 Gay Rights March on Washington, a number of participants were asked how they defined a family. A young lesbian couple pointed to their adopted sons as evidence of their family status. One group of marchers said "family" could be a man and woman, man and man, or woman and woman. Another group included various combinations—for example, two men and a woman—saying that what is right for *them* (the alleged family) was all that mattered.

"Where there is love," they said confidently, "there is a family."[42] (So if love, for whatever reason, dies, the family relationship dies as well? If parents stop loving their children, can they, under this new definition, throw their kids out?)

The real question is not whether there is love. The question is whether love *by itself* should qualify people to undo centuries of traditional and theological understanding of the term *family* to make it accommodate them and their values.

To illustrate the importance of definition, let's look at the concept of the church of Jesus Christ. It is defined in

Ephesians 1 as women and men who, having been born again by the Spirit of God through faith in Christ, are now the visible members of His body on earth. The church, then, is the body of Christ.

The church also has problems. Let's assume (and it shouldn't be hard) that the body of Christ is not functioning the way it was meant to. Suppose a panel of experts convened to discuss solutions to the church's problems, and suppose one of the experts offered the following:

> You know, there are plenty of nice people who are not Christians, but who do have some sort of faith, and who'd love to be part of the church. They could do the work of the church; why, some of them could do it better than some Christians do! Besides, the church obviously isn't functioning well in its present state. Why not redefine it to include not only born-again Christians, but also people of other faiths or nonbelievers who have faith in themselves, and who want to be recognized as part of the church? As I see it, wherever there's any kind of faith, there's the church!

A nice, poetic idea, but a *wrong* idea. Faith alone saves nobody—the One we have faith in, Jesus Christ, defines us as Christians, not just faith itself. And if a person's faith is not specifically in Christ, then he is not a part of Christ's body. That does not mean he's not a wonderful person with much to offer; it does not mean he's not deeply loved and valued by God. It simply means that, by his status as a non-Christian, he cannot truly be part of the body of Christ.

If the experts decided to redefine the church to include the non-Christian, that still would not make him a part of the church *in God's sight.* It *would,* though, weaken the witness and effectiveness of the church in general. Reconceptualized to include virtually anyone, the church could hardly preach the gospel; why bother with messy concepts like atonement and judgment if anyone with any kind of faith can now be called "the church"? And so the church, now watered down by re-definition, would no longer have the impact it was meant to have.

I suggest that this is true of the family, too. Redefining it to accommodate same-sex couples will never make them a family *in God's sight.* It will, though, weaken the effectiveness of the family in general. Standards such as monogamy and fidelity will have to change when the qualifications for "family" change, to make room for a whole new concept.

That's because the redefinition of "family" won't stop with same-sex couples. Just as the gay rights movement is now a platform for sadomasochists, transsexuals, and bisexuals (and in some cases, pedophiles), so these same groups can be expected to jump on the marriage bandwagon once the gays have opened the door.

With "love" as the standard for the "new family," any one of these groups, and other groups as well, can claim to love their partners. Logically, then, bisexual trios, a man and a transsexual, an adult and a child, and a "master" with his "sex slave" should be able to claim family status. Is this what gays want when they clamor for same-sex marriages? I doubt it. But it is the inevitable result of tampering with a God-given model.

When studies confirm that boys raised without fathers have higher rates of impulsivity and antisocial behavior;[43] when children have a better chance of success when both mother and father are present in their homes;[44] when a 1987 study of violent rapists shows that 60 percent of them came from single-parent homes;[45] when 75 percent of teenage suicides come from broken homes; and when girls raised without fathers are shown to be sexually active sooner in life and at higher risks of having children out of wedlock;[46] *can we deny the need children have for a mother and a father?*

At this point, lesbian or gay male couples might argue that they, too, can provide a safe family environment, and that as responsible, hardworking citizens, they will instill good values in their children. For the sake of argument, let's assume they are right. Suppose they remain monogamous and stay together for a lifetime, adopting and raising children in a safe, loving environment. Many heterosexual couples are unable to do the same. Doesn't that prove that we should, as the gay Christian movement asks us to, redefine "family" to include them?

No, because the question assumes that if something *works*, it must be *right*, or that if something does not match the *ideal*, yet still produces *good results*, then the ideal should be modified.

Certainly a moderate, responsible gay couple could provide a better home life than, say, an abusive heterosexual couple who beat their children or abuse drugs. But that's pitting the best-case gay scenario against the worst-case heterosexual scenario. We might just as well say that, because a responsible, loving single mother is better equipped to raise children than an irresponsible, unloving couple, then single motherhood is, in general, just as good as a two-parent home.

But it isn't. The ideal situation is still a two-parent home. Just because some two-parent homes are unhealthy does not mean the two-parent ideal should be changed.

The answer to family problems is to correct the problems, not redefine the family. No matter how benign a homosexual couple may be, if you compare what the average same-sex couple has to offer with the average opposite-sex couple, the opposite-sex couple will win out, because they include a mother *and* father.

Some feel that homosexual couples are less than ideal as parents because of their homosexuality. I would argue that it's not just their homosexuality that makes them less than ideal; it's their *sameness*. Two men or two women together—whether as a homosexual couple or as roommates or friends—cannot give a child what a heterosexual couple can. Children need the influence of *both* a man *and* woman; anything less may be good to a point, but never ideal. And to be of any real use, a standard must represent what is ideal, not what is good to a point.

Dr. Dennis Praeger, founder and president of the Micah Center for Ethical Monotheism, gives us some insight into the development of this standard in his excellent essay, "Why Judaism Rejected Homosexuality":

> When Judaism demanded that all sexual activity be channeled into marriage, it changed the world. The subsequent dominance of the Western world can be attributed to the sexual revolution initiated by Judaism and later carried forward by Christianity. This revolution consisted of *forcing the sexual genie into the marital bottle*[47] (emphasis added).

Dr. Praeger refers to the "utterly wild" nature of human sexuality which, when unbridled, expresses itself in every conceivable coupling and combination. The Torah called for a civilizing influence, creating and protecting the notion of a family by rigid definitions and roles. In so doing, God decreed that sexuality conform to a specific standard; the standard cannot yield to accommodate sexuality.

This is why, when gays claim their sexuality is "natural" to them, I am inclined to say, "So what?" *Natural* (in the subjective sense, as in "natural to me") does not mean *right*; the created *intent* for sexual expression must dictate what forms of sexual expression are acceptable. So if people choose to pursue their "natural" sexual inclinations, we may grant their right to do so. But we cannot grant their demand that the standard for marriage and family be revised to suit what is natural *to them*, yet unnatural *in fact*.

If the church is to be, as Jesus said, the salt of the earth (a preserver of right standards and truth) and the light of the world (a guide to righteousness and life), then her responsibility to the world is to love it as Christ did by speaking truth to it, not by accommodating its demands. Nor can she join its assaults on standards of marriage clearly spelled out in the Bible. Dr. Praeger, writing about these assaults, understood the reasons some groups have for making them. "What I have not understood," he adds, "is why Jews or Christians would join the assaults. I do now. They do not know what is at stake. At stake is our civilization."[48]

When I was very young, I tragically walked into a series of situations that would shape, to a large extent, my sexual future. I had been warned about certain areas of my city where men "wanted" young boys. Curious and hungry for whatever "wanted" meant, I visited these spots and, on several occasions, was sexually molested.

Thank God, my family, who knew nothing of this, upheld a standard of decency that kept me from ever believing that what happened to me was "beautiful." Although it resulted in untold confusion and wild indulgences, at least I still retained the ideals I had been taught at home. They served as a compass by which I could, when I decided to, return to my moral base.

Years later, as a teenager, I began a series of encounters with adult men from other cities. I met these men through contacts in an underground newspaper. (I looked quite a bit older than I really was; most of these men took me to be in my twenties.) Shortly afterwards, I first heard the gospel, and with it I heard a strong call to turn away from fornication. If the church I attended hadn't maintained biblical standards, that call would never have come.

When, in 1984, as a backslidden Christian, I finally questioned whether I'd been right in accepting the gay Christian movement's beliefs, the church I returned to still held to its standards. Those standards made me uncomfortable, but it was that discomfort that lead me to repent and seek a better life. In the process I learned entirely different ways of relating to men, met and married a beautiful woman, and, by the time this book is published, will have become a father.

None of this would have been available to me if my church had not, through clear biblical teaching, provided guidance from one way of living to another. If it had lowered its standards of marriage and sexual behavior to accommodate the gay Christian movement, I cannot imagine where, and in what condition, I would be today.

Resisting the gay Christian movement was obviously worth the bother. It still is.

3

How It Began:
The Gay Rights
Movement
(1950–1969)

"Nobody sat down and conspired to create the problems our society faces. They were simply allowed to happen."
— Rabbi Daniel Lapin

Major denominations ordaining homosexuals, priests and clergy presiding over same-sex weddings, sanctuaries invaded by boisterous gay activists, debates over homosexuality ripping congregations apart, who would have guessed we'd ever reach such a point in church history?

A vigorous debate between Christians and homosexuals should not be surprising in and of itself. If Dennis Praeger is right when he says the Judeo-Christian ethic is responsible for the western world's disapproval of homosexuality,[1] then conflicts between the church and the gay rights movement are not only understandable, they're inevitable. (While acceptance of homosexuality in ancient cultures is well documented,[2] the past 2,000 years of western thought have, by and large, rejected it,[3] and the influence of both the Old and New Testaments can be credited for that.[4])

So the tension we see today between Christians and gay rights advocates is no surprise. It is a clash between two opposing philosophies: one confining sexual behavior to a specific standard, the other fighting for something much broader. They can hardly be expected to coexist peacefully. Our culture's acceptance (not total, but to a high degree) of homosexuality should not surprise us, either, since the Judeo-Christian ethic has been spurned in many ways for the past three decades.

What *is* surprising, though, is that we have reached a point where these ethics are not only being challenged, they're being rewritten as well. To better understand how they are being rewritten, *and why*, we need to first review the evolution of the gay rights movement in America, the subsequent development of the gay Christian movement, and the church's response to both.

"Do I *Really* Need to Know About Gay History?"

The more you know about a group—what they've experienced, where they've been, what events have shaped their beliefs—the more effectively you can respond to them. And while learning about their background, you just might develop a more insightful, sympathetic attitude toward them.

My favorite author, Charles Dickens, was a master of sympathetic insight. His stories feature characters guilty of horrible deeds, but when he explains their backgrounds, we can't help but feel some pity for them, even as we despise their actions.

The miserly old Scrooge in *A Christmas Carol* can't be excused for his cruelty to the poor. But his own bleak childhood helps us to understand what hardened his heart. Miss Havisham, the demented spinster of *Great Expectations*, appalls us when she uses her adopted daughter to hurt men of all ages. But when we learn how she was jilted in her own youth, we feel some compassion for her. When the peasant masses in *A Tale of Two*

Cities rise up with unreasonable fury against all aristocrats, Dickens reminds us of the abuse they endured, and so we understand them better. We hate *what* they did, but we see *why* they did it.

The better we understand the events that lead a group of people to behave in a certain way, the better we are able to deal with them. For that reason, before confronting the gay Christian movement, it is important to know the elements that gave rise to it.

Movements are not monolithic, by the way. Members of any movement have some common, general beliefs, and some different ideas as well. Ask a feminist, for example, what the priorities of the women's movement are and she may tell you they are equal pay and affirmative action; ask another feminist the same question and she might say "reproductive freedom." Two different feminists, two separate priorities. Yet both will tell you their general commitment is to women's rights.

The gay rights and the gay Christian movement are similar. As each has grown, its members have become more diverse in their beliefs and approaches, while retaining some common, general goals. Compare the gay rights movement of 1969, with its emphasis on demonstrations and "coming out of the closet," to that of 1990, and you will see a more diversified, sophisticated, sometimes even fragmented group. The same can be said of the gay Christian movement.

So it is not wise to assume that all members of a group or movement believe exactly the same thing. But you can, in most cases, gain a general idea of what they stand for. To do that, it is best to examine the statements and actions of their leaders, the body of writing they have produced, and the common themes running through each. Those three elements can provide an accurate picture of a group's general views, while allowing for some differences in its membership. With that in mind, let's take a look at the development of both the gay rights and the gay Christian movements, and the church's response to each over the past four decades.

The Early Years

Although there were some challenges during the first half of the century to the common belief that homosexuality was unnatural,[5] there was no visible homosexual movement in America until the 1950s. This is not to say there was no homosexual *subculture* before then; there was, and it thrived. But the origin of the gay rights movement can be traced to 1950, with the founding of the Mattachine Society (for homosexuals of both sexes) and the Daughters of Bilitis (a lesbian organization).[6]

Both groups were conservative in their approach. "Evolution, not Revolution" was the means Mattachine sought to use in achieving its goals; the Daughters of Bilitis showed similar restraint.[7] The movement's goals were to reform the public image of the homosexual (from "pervert" to respectable citizen), to see homosexual acts decriminalized, and to see homosexuals gain "full participation" in American life.[8] By gaining the support of psychiatrists, scientists, and clergy, they hoped to achieve these goals through reason and public discussion.

It is interesting to note that in 1955 (five years after the founding of Mattachine), the first serious challenge to the Bible's condemnation of homosexuality was published. Dr. Derrick S. Bailey, an Anglican theologian who argued for the acceptance of homosexuality,[9] published *Homosexuality and the Western Christian Tradition.* In this book Bailey claimed that the destruction of Sodom in Genesis 19 came about not because of homosexual acts, but because of inhospitality. This uncommon interpretation of Genesis 19 would be repeated for decades within the gay Christian movement.

The quiet approach the early gay rights movement was taking met with little opposition from churches. This was not an indication of approval (though some liberal theologians were already sympathizing with Mattachine's goals), but since most Christians were unaware of these low-profile groups, there was little mention of homosexuality from America's pulpits. That was yet to come.

One exception was a group of 11 Quakers who were at least aware of homosexuality, if not the homosexual movement, and who took a friendly view of it. The Literary Committee of the Friends Home Service in England published, in 1963, a pamphlet on sexuality that reads like a 30-year forerunner to the controversial Presbyterian report of the 1990s. It allowed for premarital sex, approved of adultery in some cases, and viewed homosexuality as acceptable.[10] While not reflecting the official Quaker view at the time, and certainly not influencing Christian or secular thought on homosexuality in the early 1960s, the pamphlet stands out as an early milestone in the gay Christian movement.

The philosophy of the Mattachines and Daughters of Bilitis, meanwhile, was gradually evolving. Initially, some leaders in both groups considered their own homosexuality to be an illness, or at least a serious handicap. While supporting fair treatment for homosexuals, these leaders (themselves homosexual, or "homophile," as they were often called then) still believed their sexual state was less than ideal.[11] Early debates within the movement, in fact, centered on whether or not homosexuals should support psychiatry, since its general view was antihomosexual. Some thought mental health specialists could be valuable allies in their fight against unfair treatment. Others, who felt perfectly comfortable with their homosexuality, viewed those same psychiatrists as enemies needing to be challenged.

The homosexual movement from 1950 to 1965, then, was marked by a struggle for self-definition and understanding.

From "Please Treat Gays Fairly" to "Gay Is Good"

By 1965 psychiatry was seen by gay leaders much the same way that the church is viewed by them today—

as the primary institution frustrating the goals of the homosexual movement.

That same year, the movement produced a statement of gay pride that rejected the opinions of psychiatry and society. In essence, it said that homosexuality is *not* an illness, that solidarity among homosexuals is an important tool in reaching their goal of equality with heterosexuals, and that tactics more aggressive than public discussion and education were needed if they were ever to achieve their goals.[12]

A third published argument for the pro-gay theology came out two years later. Wainwright Churchill's *Homosexual Behavior Among Males* (Hawthorne Books, 1967) called for a "new morality in the sexual sphere," repeated Bailey's explanation of Sodom's destruction, and praised Bailey and the Friends' report for their groundbreaking conclusions.[13] Like its predecessors, Churchill's book was not written by a self-identified gay Christian. But, also like its predecessors, it laid more groundwork for the gay Christian movement.

The call for more aggressive tactics was answered twice in 1968, when homosexual activists demonstrated at the convention of the American Medical Association (AMA) in San Francisco, and at Columbia University's College of Physicians and Surgeons, where a panel on homosexuality was convening.[14] Inspired in no small part by the civil rights movement, they used leaflets, protests, and appeals to the public's sense of fairness to make their points.

At both the AMA convention and Columbia University, activists demanded participation in future professional conventions and discussions on homosexuality, arguing that it was time that "they [the professionals] stopped talking *about* us and started being with us."[15] Even if not entirely successful, it was the beginning of empowerment and, as Ronald Bayer says, *healing*: "Though not necessarily couched in terms of violence, action and rebellion were seen as antidotes to the

shame, self-doubt, and self-hatred that had been im-
posed upon homosexuals by society."[16]

Apparently, then, public demonstrations not only
made a statement—*they felt good!* That good, empow-
ered feeling would be reported by gay activists again and
again. But the true 1968 milestone for the gay Christian
movement occurred much more quietly than the demonstrations at Columbia and San Francisco.

The First Pro-Gay Denomination

On October 6, 1968, 12 people responded to an ad
placed in *The Advocate* (a gay-oriented newspaper) inviting them to worship in a newly formed church for homosexuals. The ad was placed by a 28-year-old former
Pentecostal minister named Troy Perry.

Nearly 30 years later, Reverend Perry is still one of
the gay Christian movement's most influential leaders.
As such, he is of interest to anyone hoping to understand pro-gay Christians.

The denomination Perry founded that October after-
noon—the Universal Fellowship of Metropolitan Community Churches (UFMCC)—is, by his own claim, "the
largest organization touching the lives of gays and lesbians in the world."[17] Nearly 300 UFMCC congregations
exist worldwide, and with social and political action encouraged among its members, Perry's claim about
UFMCC's influence is probably true.

In his books *The Lord Is My Shepherd and He Knows
I'm Gay* (Nash Publishing, 1972) and *Don't Be Afraid
Anymore* (St. Martin's Press, 1990), Perry recounts the
early experiences, both sexual and spiritual, that
shaped his thinking. The oldest of five boys, he was
raised by his doting mother Edith in a religious environment. After his father's death in a car accident, he sur-
vived abuse from a violent stepfather who battered Edith
and evidently arranged for one of his friends to rape 13-
year-old Troy as punishment for coming to his mother's
defense.[18]

He found refuge in church and was especially attracted to Pentecostalism. His ministerial gifts showed up early. By age 15 he was a licensed Baptist preacher; by his late teens he was a paid evangelist with the charismatic Church of God. Shortly thereafter he married and took a pastorate in the latter denomination. Having been aware of homosexual attractions the better part of his life, Perry involved himself with other young men, both before and after his marriage, and was eventually excommunicated from the Church of God and divorced from his wife.

Years later, after joining the gay subculture, he was moved by the distress of one of his friends who had been jailed for simply being in a gay bar (a common occurrence at the time). Perry recalls the conversation with this friend, which led to his sense of calling to start a gay church:

"We're just a bunch of dirty queers and nobody cares about dirty queers!"

"Somebody cares," I said.

"Who?"

"God cares."

Tony uttered a terrible laugh. "No, Troy. What do you mean, 'God cares'? Be serious!"[19]

That night he conceived the idea of a church for gay people to show them that God did indeed care. A year later he founded the church. Today, the denomination springing from Perry's living room is represented in at least eight foreign countries and throughout most of the United States.

These early stirrings of the gay rights movement, and the gay Christian movement, were quiet and subtle. From the 1950s to the late 60s, the gay rights movement grew and defined itself by saying, "We are not sick, we want validation, and we are prepared to fight for it."

The gay Christian movement, even more than the gay rights movement, was in its infancy. With scattered support from a handful of liberal churches, it adopted a self-definition similar to that of the gay rights movement, with an addendum: "God loves and accepts us just as we are; *and* homosexuality is okay with Him."

As they entered 1969, both movements were unaware of a coming earthquake that would eventually propel them into the nation's consciousness.

4

War:
The Gay Rights
Movement
(1969-1979)

"Be proud of what you are, man! And if it takes riots or even guns to show them what we are, well, that's the only language that pigs understand."
>—Gay activist at meeting following the 1969 Stonewall riots

"This is war, and anything goes."
>— Executive Director of the National Gay and Lesbian Task Force

*I*t happened without forethought, warning, or plan. No identifiable leaders were involved in it; no call to arms got it going. But it inflamed and, to an extent, redefined the homosexual movement. Revered by gays as the turning point from which they must never retreat, it is celebrated annually in gay pride rallies and parades. It was called a riot by the local press when it happened. Today, it's known as Stonewall.

Reviewing the headlines from 1969, a reader could miss Stonewall altogether. It gets more press today than it did when it occurred, possibly because gay-related issues received little coverage back then. Or maybe the other newsworthy items of 1969—Woodstock, the Manson family murders, the first man on the moon—drowned it out in retrospect. At any rate, it's impossible to review the gay rights movement without giving space to the Stonewall riots.

In the early morning hours of June 28, nine plainclothes detectives entered a gay bar in New York's Greenwich Village called the Stonewall Inn. Intending to close the bar for selling liquor without a license, they ejected the nearly 200 patrons who were inside, then arrested the bartender, three transvestite customers, and a doorman. But when they escorted their charges outside, they found that an angry crowd had gathered on the sidewalk. Someone—exactly who and why are matters of discussion to this day—threw something at them, and within minutes the crowd, which eventually swelled to nearly 400, also began hurling rocks and bottles at the police. The officers retreated and barricaded themselves in the bar until backup enforcements arrived, and within 45 minutes the rioting stopped.[1]

The scene repeated itself the next night when another crowd gathered outside the Stonewall, chanting, "Legalize gay bars!" and "Gay is good!" Fires were started, and bottles were again thrown at police who battled with the demonstrators for two hours before they finally dispersed. Four nights later, yet another gay mob—this one nearly 500 strong—took to the streets in Greenwich Village, marching and shouting slogans.

Exactly what prompted Stonewall is uncertain. Some rather silly ideas have been proposed, one of which is that the recent death of gay icon Judy Garland had put homosexuals in a foul mood.[2] A better explanation would consider some of the social forces at work in the late 60s.

Vietnam, campus unrest, and the relatively young civil rights movement fueled scores of public demonstrations so that by 1969, a group of angry protestors was a common enough sight. The times were almost wildly anti-authority; government was the dreaded "Establishment," adults over 30 were not to be trusted, campus administrators were openly defied, and police were written off as "pigs." (The Stonewall mob, in fact, chanted "pigs," among other things, while they pelted the police with rocks and bottles.) Everything traditional was subject to question; it was honorable to challenge the norm. In this context both Stonewall and the aggressive new tone it gave to the gay rights movement make perfect sense.

By then, many homosexuals saw themselves as a mistreated minority. Too often, they were right. Assaulted for no other reason than the sickness of people who hated them,[3] ignored at times in the legal process,[4] and sometimes unreasonably harassed by police,[5] they were, collectively, *angry*. The Stonewall riots gave public expression to their pent-up anger; the public expression, in turn, inspired a new defiance among gays.[6]

Immediately after the rioting, homosexual activist groups began forming, first in New York, then nationwide. Plans for future demonstrations, political action, and cultural reform began to take shape. Within months, Gay Power (a term birthed shortly after Stonewall) took its place alongside its cousins of the 60s: Flower Power, Power to the People, and Black Power.[7]

The homosexual population entered the 1970s with a fresh sense of unity and definition. *U.S. News and World Report* writer Erica Goode spells out the post-Stonewall elements which, at that time, gave both the gay rights and the gay Christian movements their core of strength:

> The idea that sexual orientation was an important characteristic, that it *set a group of people apart, defining them as different in some essential way,* and a realization, among those attracted towards members of their own gender, that there were others like them, facing

the same difficulties and concerns[8] (emphasis added).

The construction of a "gay identity" was crucial to this, so gay activists began educating the public as to how they should view homosexuality. No longer was homosexuality to be seen as a condition or a behavior; it was now to be considered a fundamental part of one's makeup, no less permanent than skin color or gender. By that reasoning, any objection to homosexuality now placed the objector in the same category as a racial bigot or a "sexist." By shifting the focus of homosexuality from *behavior* to *identity*, the gay rights and gay Christian movements gained new ground by "gradually turning," as Goode explains, "what had been a series of sexual sins into an identity, a way of being."[9]

Stonewall was a declaration of war. Demonstrations would continue to play a key role, but war involves more than hand-to-hand combat; there are troops to mobilize, alliances to forge, and strategies to be laid. Reviewing the written accounts of gay rights meetings in 1969 and the early 1970s,[10] the strategy gay leaders seemed to agree on was threefold:

1. Encourage all homosexuals to "come out of the closet" and declare their sexuality as a key part of their identity.

2. Form and strengthen alliances with groups and individuals sympathetic to the gay cause.

3. Confront people or institutions who resisted the gay cause.

Each strategy was a mandate for action. And as the gay rights movement acted on each mandate, the gay Christian movement was never far behind.

Mandate One: "Come Out!"

The first mandate—encouraging gays to "come out" and identify themselves by their sexual desires—was furthered when the first anniversary of the Stonewall riots was celebrated in New York City in June 1970.

Nearly 10,000 lesbians and gay men—easily the largest public gathering of homosexuals in American history—marched down Sixth Avenue and gathered in Central Park. "Out of the Closets! Into the Streets!" they chanted, beginning a yearly tradition of celebrating Stonewall that continues today.

As the gay rights movement got more press, men and women who kept their homosexual longings a secret (either for moral reasons or fear of retaliation) heard the invitation to "come out" and "accept who you truly are." It was an attractive invitation, especially to Christians who battled homosexual temptations. In their conservative churches they were hearing little to help them overcome their struggles; homosexuality was not, by and large, discussed. They were in a silent battle with themselves, and it was hellishly lonely. So when the gay rights movement offered them support, through a community of people who understood what it meant to be homosexual, they were interested. The only obstacle was their faith—how could they choose between being gay or being Christian?

The gay Christian movement removed the hurdle by telling them there was no choice to be made—gay *AND* Christian was now an option! They responded in droves, some by leaving their more conservative churches to join the Metropolitan Community Church, others by seeking out "gay-friendly" denominations. And as they did, the gay Christian movement, emulating the gay rights movement of 1969, stepped into the sunlight.

Gay Christian material began showing up in secular and Christian bookstores.[11] In 1972 Troy Perry published his autobiographical *The Lord Is My Shepherd and He Knows I'm Gay.* Four years later Malcolm Boyd, a re-knowned Episcopalian priest and best-selling author, openly declared his homosexuality, documented in *Take Off the Mask* (St. Martin's Press). Tom Horner, another Episcopalian priest, submitted his revision of every biblical text on homosexuality in his book, *Jonathan Loved David* (Westminster Press).

Most notable of all the gay Christian literature in this period was Letha Scanzoni and Virginia Ramey Mollenkott's *Is the Homosexual My Neighbor?* (Harper and Row, 1978). Prior to the publication of this book, pro-gay writing (even that which found its way into religious bookstores) went largely unnoticed by conservative Christians. But now, for the first time in its history, the gay Christian movement had produced an explanation of its view that caught the attention of evangelicals and fundamentalists. Combining new interpretations of Scripture with earnest (if unconvincing) arguments, the book was praised by secular and Christian sources, including *Christianity Today, The Christian Century, The Journal of the Evangelical Theological Society,* and *The Christian Ministry.* Endorsements from such respected Christian publications was proof that the gay Christian movement was gaining momentum and credibility.

Further proof was seen in the growing visibility and influence of the Universal Fellowship of Metropolitan Community Churches (UFMCC). Troy Perry, the Fellowship's moderator, became internationally recognized within years of founding the UFMCC. In 1972 he addressed a London convention on homosexuality; author and theologian Norman Pittenger attended and gave Perry's speech his approval.[12] Two years later Perry assisted the Australian "Campaign Against Moral Pressure."[13] The next year he was one of 80 leaders invited to meet Governor Jimmy Carter during his bid for the Democratic nomination, after which he led a "gays for Carter" campaign.[14] In 1977 he was invited to Carter's White House to present, along with other gay leaders, his concerns on homosexuality in America.[15]

UFMCC ministers, meanwhile, gained increased exposure through talk shows and news conferences, and Metropolitan Community Churches sprang up around the country. The gay Christian movement was successfully following the first mandate of the gay rights movement. It was out of the closet, proclaiming homo-sexuality as a God-given gift, and encouraging all homosexuals to do likewise.

Mandate Two: Form Alliances

The gay Christian movement also followed the second mandate of the gay rights movement by forming alliances with its sympathizers. Troy Perry was (and is) especially good at this. When the Los Angeles Metropolitan Community Church was destroyed by arson in 1973, he took out an ad in *Variety* magazine soliciting donations to rebuild the sanctuary; a generous response followed. When he openly fasted for 16 days in front of the Federal Building in Los Angeles, in protest of a ballot initiative restricting gay schoolteachers, he raised $100,00 from supporters across the country. And when he spoke at a fund-raiser targeting the same initiative, he was hailed by the likes of John Travolta, Burt Lancaster, and Cher.[16]

Alliances the mainstream church might envy—but will probably never attain—have come easily to the gay Christian movement. The news and entertainment industry, both highly supportive of the gay rights movement, have forged a tidy bond with the gay Christian movement as well. I remember seeing signed portraits of Phyllis Diller and Mae West hanging at the Los Angeles Metropolitan Community Church. Troy Perry, the church's founder, counts Phil Donahue as one of his friends.[17] When Mel White announced his homosexuality in 1993, media giants such as Barbara Walters and Larry King gave him generous coverage.[18] Shirley MacLaine, at an AIDS fund-raiser, offered her blessing to a gay minister while Stevie Wonder stood by.[19] Support from Hollywood is, in fact, a given among the gay churches.

(This Hollywood support shows itself on the local as well as national level. Once, during a rather formal Metropolitan Community Church banquet, I found myself decked out in a tuxedo, sweating my way through a piano solo while Martha Raye, seated five feet away, beamed at me.)

Alliances with churches were also formed after Stonewall. On July 16, 1969, just weeks after the riots, the second "Gay Power" strategy meeting was held in a local Episcopal church.[20] Two years later the United Church of Christ ordained the first openly gay minister in a major denomination.[21] And in January 1977, the Episcopal Church of New York ordained an openly lesbian woman.[22]

Gay networks soon developed within major denominations, where they operated with or without official church sanction. In 1974, Lutherans Concerned was founded for gay Lutherans and their supporters. Two years later, Affirmation was born among the United Methodists as an organization for "Lesbian and Gay Concerns." Integrity (an Episcopalian gay group), Dignity (for Catholic homosexuals), and Kinship (the pro-gay Seventh Day Adventist group) established themselves in their respective denominations. Conference for Catholic Lesbians, Friends (Quakers) for Lesbian and Gay Concerns, and the United Church of Christ Coalition for Gay and Lesbian Concerns did likewise.[23]

With its visibility growing, alliances with prominent individuals secured, and groups and churches in place, the gay Christian movement was equipped to follow the gay rights movement's next, and most dramatic, mandate.

Mandate Three: Confrontation

Before 1977 there were few clashes between the gay rights movement and the conservative church. Aside from minor skirmishes—the Daughters of Bilitis staged a demonstration at St. Patrick's Cathedral in 1971, for instance[24]—public conflicts between the two groups were rare.

Gay leaders knew the conservative church disapproved of homosexuality, but in the early years of their movement, they had other concerns. If society was unsympathetic to their cause, they felt, it was largely because homosexuality was considered an illness. To change society's view, it was necessary to first change the view of the institution responsible for labeling them "sick." Thus the American Psychiatric Association (APA) became the target of relentless, well-organized gay protests, beginning in 1968 and lasting five years. In 1973 the efforts of gay leadership paid off: The APA deleted homosexuality from its list of disorders. (See chapter 7.)

After the APA changed its position, gays were armed with fresh ideological boldness. They could now confront politicians, educators, and even the federal government with a new approach. If American psychiatry no longer said homosexuality was abnormal, they reasoned, then antisodomy laws and restrictions on military service for homosexuals should be abolished. They further demanded, based on the APA's decision, that civil rights protection be afforded to gays, and that schools teach students to regard homosexuality as normal.[25]

They demanded more than they got, but they got a great deal. By 1976, some 15 states had removed antisodomy laws from their books, and 33 cities had enacted civil rights codes protecting homosexuals. The American Bar Association, the American Medical Association, and the American Psychological Association officially supported decriminalizing homosexual behavior, and the United States Civil Service Commission stopped excluding gays from federal employment.[26]

These advances were not entirely ignored by the conservative church. In 1974 the New York Catholic Archdiocese openly opposed civil rights codes for gays.[27] Two years later, a national coalition of conservative ministries formed to help those who wanted to overcome their homosexuality.[28] But, just as the gays felt that confronting the church was not yet a priority, so the church saw no pressing need to confront the gay rights movement. Most likely, despite its progress, conservative Christians did not yet feel that the movement had encroached on their own rights.

One exception was a Christian entertainer whose name, whether justly or not, would come to symbolize confrontation between gays and Christians.

The Anita Bryant Campaign

In January 1977, the Board of Commissioners of Dade County, Florida, approved an ordinance prohibiting discrimination based on sexual orientation. Local Christian leaders opposed the ordinace, seeing it as an official endorsement of homosexuality. One of them was Anita Bryant, a 37-year-old singer, author, and former Miss America. When asked to spearhead a campaign to repeal the Dade County ordinance, she accepted.[29] She announced her intentions and began mobilizing support, and the press stepped up its coverage of her efforts, with good reason. While Dade County's gay rights ordinance was not unique (similar laws were already on the books in other states), it was the first one officially opposed by a celebrity figure—a *female* celebrity, at that—who was also a Christian, a recording artist, and a former beauty queen to boot! The story was irresistible.

Anita Bryant's campaign propelled the Christian viewpoint of homosexuality into the national spotlight, where it could be examined and hotly debated. Miss Bryant was interviewed and editorialized by newspapers, magazines, and network television. On national talk shows she quoted Scripture and explained her moral opposition to gay rights. Gay spokesmen responded, at times furiously, and soon the gloves were off. Accusations and wild exaggerations were thrown out by gays and, sadly, by a few Christians as well.

Gays publicly compared Anita Bryant to Hitler.[30] She was accused of inciting violence against them,[31] causing them to lose their jobs,[32] and threatening human rights in general.[33] Her name became a rallying cry among gays, a common enemy who united them.

Unfortunately, as Christian leaders jumped into the discussion, they, too, made some irresponsible remarks. On religious television and radio programs, gays were often referred to as potential child molesters, with no studies or facts to back such claims. They were said to "recruit" others into homosexuality, to be worthy of imprisonment, and to be insatiable in their lust. It was not enough to simply object to homosexuality; it seemed necessary (in many cases) to paint lurid pictures of homosexuals as well. And so the wall between gays and the conservative church shot up, stacked with hostility and mutual distrust.

None of this was lost on the gay Christian movement which, perhaps even more than the general gay population, saw the Bryant campaign as an affront to their very identity. Not only was Miss Bryant condemning homosexuality, but she was using the Bible—the same Bible they claimed to believe in—as the moral authority behind her crusade. She emphasized, perhaps more than any public figure ever had, the chasm between "homosexual" and "Christian." Those who claimed to be both were compelled to defend their position. And so, in the spring of 1977, the gay Christian movement followed the third mandate of the gay rights movement: confrontation.

As it turned out, gay Christian leaders were in a better position to confront Bryant than nonreligious gays, because they spoke her language. When she quoted Bible verses, they could respond with Scripture as well; when she claimed divine guidance, they could do the same.

To Christians who were biblically literate, the pro-gay religious arguments were easy to see through. But to the general public, many of whom would be voting on gay rights bills in Florida and elsewhere, the gay Christian approach confused the issue. After all, if both sides claimed to be Bible-believing Christians doing God's will, how was the average citizen to know who was right? Troy Perry, explaining why he needed to debate

Bryant's supporters on television, put it well: "Our enemies are taking the language of Scripture and running wild with it. Nobody's talking classroom civics in Miami—this is a religious issue! And I speak the language!"[34]

Despite considerable pro-gay efforts, in June 1977 the voters in Dade County repealed the gay rights ordinance by a 69 percent to 30 percent margin. Anita Bryant claimed victory, and rightfully so. Not only had she fought in the public arena and won, but she had broken new ground while doing so. She had taken an unpopular stand without wavering. In retrospect, we might ask why more Christian men were not willing to oppose the gay movement as bravely as she did. She faced a media that was often hostile, endured innumerable insults, and set a new standard for Christian activism.

The battle over Dade County, though, was far from over. It simply transferred itself to cities across the nation, where similar gay rights ordinances were being considered, debated, and voted on. In a sense, the Anita Bryant campaign was a turning point for Christians and gays.

It marked a new awareness, among Christians, of homosexuality and the demands of the gay rights movement. Just as Bryant had, in her words, a "live and let live" attitude until the Dade County ordinance forced her to take a stand, so the church, in the aftermath of Dade County's battle, realized that a "great transformation" had taken place in the homosexual movement: "No longer content with mere tolerance, gay activist groups sought social acceptance, and the legitimization of homosexuality as an alternative sexual orientation."[35]

"Social acceptance" included laws prohibiting discrimination against homosexuals in housing and employment, and pro-gay education programs in public schools. Goals such as these could hardly be ignored by Christian businessmen, who now realized they might face lawsuits by not hiring openly homosexual employees. Christian landlords, forced to rent to gay couples despite their religious objections, were equally concerned. And parents of all faiths, envisioning their children being taught the "normalcy" of homosexuality, were understandably alarmed. Just as Dade County had put the Christian view of homosexuality in the public spotlight, so it had also displayed the gay agenda in the same glare. It, too, was scrutinized, debated, and reacted to.

As a result, Christian resistance to the gay rights movement increased, at local and national levels, from 1977 onward. Whatever the outcome, each new battle found conservative Christians confronting, or being confronted by, the gay Christian movement.

In 1978 California State Senator John Briggs sponsored an unsuccessful ballot initiative to restrict public school teachers from endorsing homosexuality. His primary and most visible opponent was Troy Perry.[36] Dr. Beverly LaHaye founded Concerned Women of America (CWA), a formidable women's organization frequently at odds with gay causes. She would later be castigated by Mel White as one of his favorite "homophobic radio or television personalities"[37] who "uses her own genteel brand of homophobia" to mobilize CWA.[38] Dr. Jerry Falwell organized the Moral Majority in 1979 to combat, among other things, gay rights and abortion.[39] His subsequent clashes with both the gay rights and gay Christian movements are legendary.[40]

As gay rights battles were fought across the country, gay Christian spokespersons jousted with conservatives in television and radio debates. Each appearance gave new exposure to the gay Christian viewpoint, and exposure was a plus for the movement. When the pro-gay interpretation of the Bible was argued in public, sympathetic journalists and talk show hosts picked it up and repeated it before national audiences. "That's just *your* interpretation of those Bible verses" became a common response from the likes of Phil Donahue when conservative studio guests explained their Bible-based objections to homosexuality. "There is a new way of looking at them, you know!"

Thus gay Christians spread their philosophy, both through their own materials and through their media allies. If success is measured by expansion and visibility, the gay Christian movement's achievements from 1970 to 1979 are inarguable. From a fledgling population, it had grown to become an eloquent and aggressive wing of the gay rights movement. Brimming with media savvy and finding itself well-connected politically, it ended a decade of culture wars as a force to be reckoned with.

5

The Gay Christian
Movement
Comes of Age

"So there you have it. This ecclesiastical phoenix rising from the ashes of Sodom. It cannot, will not be ignored. The heterosexual Christian is now forced to declare himself and reaffirm or disregard his beliefs about what the Scriptures teach."

— Paul Morris, Ph.D.,
"Shadow of Sodom"

By 1980 there was an identifiable body of work, from a variety of sources, promoting the pro-gay theology. At least nine books, most of them published through major houses, were on the market,[1] while journals and articles debated the pro-gay position relentlessly. The gay Christian population was easy to spot as well, inside and outside mainline denominations. Gay caucuses flourished in traditional churches, while newer groups such as the Metropolitan Community Church, Evangelicals Concerned,[2] and independent gay churches continued their expansion.

With expansion came clout and, more importantly, the power of persuasion. So far, the gay rights and gay Christian movements had influenced policies in local and federal government, education,[3] the media,[4] and, of course, the American Psychiatric Association. Churches of a more liberal bent were also influenced toward a pro-gay position. Troy Perry, when explaining how easily liberal churches accepted his beliefs, made an interesting admission: "I knew I would have few if any problems with the so-called liberal churches. Liberal churches do not usually deeply involve themselves with Scripture."[5]

But the final conquest—the conservative church—remained, and remains, immune to gay persuasion for the opposite reason: conservative churches *do* involve themselves deeply with Scripture! To convince conservative Christians that God condones homosexuality, the gay Christian movement needed a rebuttal, *in conservative terms*, to the traditional biblical view. Ignoring the Bible would hardly be acceptable; attacking its authority would be even worse. For the gay Christian movement to convince its toughest critics, it needed to affirm the Bible as the ultimate authority *and* prove that the ultimate authority did not condemn homosexual behavior.

The movement hadn't yet succeeded. Troy Perry's writing, though full of interesting stories that were emotionally compelling, was doctrinally weak.[6] Scanzoni and Mollenkott spent nine chapters of *Is the Homosexual My Neighbor?* examining psychology, sociology, medical science, and personal testimonies of homosexuals who tried to change but "couldn't," yet they devoted only one chapter to a scriptural "defense" of homosexuality. Tom Horner's *Jonathan Loved David* concentrated on culture and history, then gave brief space to biblical concerns and admitted that the apostle Paul would most likely "not have looked kindly" on homosexual behavior.[7]

With its wobbly scriptural base, the gay Christian movement's growth from 1969 to 1979 is startling, considering that many of its members were from conservative church backgrounds where they were taught respect for the Bible. Yet their early writings show, instead of a well thought-out scriptural position, a sort of loosely knit resolution that could be paraphrased as follows:

> Whereas we have been mistreated and misunderstood, and whereas much of our mistreatment has come from Christian people, and whereas we tried to resist our homosexual desires but were unable to, and whereas psychologists recognize us as normal, and whereas we know God loves us and we want to continue in fellowship with Him, therefore, be it resolved that God does not condemn homosexuality.

That may have been enough for liberal believers and gay sympathizers, but conservative Christians would never buy it. So the gay Christian movement could alternately ignore conservatives or fight them (both of which they certainly did) or, better yet, meet them on their own turf with Bible-based arguments.

Such arguments would serve three purposes. First, they would provide ammunition in the escalating war that gays were fighting with groups such as Jerry Falwell's Moral Majority. Conservative religious organizations were influencing public policy; they encouraged their constituents to fight "gay rights" on biblical grounds. If the gay Christian movement could show their grounds were just as biblical, conservative Christians might lose credibility in the public's mind.

Second, persuasive biblical arguments could settle whatever self-doubts some gay Christians might be having, and encourage other Christians struggling with homosexuality to accept it as a gift and join the gay Christian ranks.

Finally, it might win some heterosexual conservative Christians over to the gay Christian camp, making valuable allies out of them. Attorney and professor F. LaGard Smith recognizes the importance of this when he writes, "Gays realize that they must deal with the whole of Scripture if they are to have any chance of convincing us—or themselves—that homosexual conduct is pleasing to God. It's a daunting task, but they set forth in confidence."[8]

That confidence was radically bolstered in September 1981, when the gay Christian movement's most impressive defense was released in bookstores around the country.

Professor John Boswell

Christianity, Social Tolerance and Homosexuality, by John Boswell, is to the gay Christian movement what *Uncle Tom's Cabin* was to the abolitionists—a reference point, the authoritative text, an inspiration. Pick up any pro-gay religious book written since 1981, or listen to a debate on homosexuality and the Bible, and quotes from Boswell are likely to abound. His is unquestionably the most comprehensive defense for a revised view of Bible verses, in both Testaments, referring to homosexuality. And while no one has provided a convincingly biblical pro-gay argument, Dr. Boswell's is the strongest effort to date.

While a professor of history at Yale University, Boswell spent ten years researching his 434-page defense for the pro-gay revision. *Christianity, Social Tolerance and Homosexuality* presents two main arguments: (1) the Christian church has not always disapproved of homosexuality, and (2) the Bible verses assumed to condemn homosexual sex do not refer to homosexuality at all, but to various other forms of immorality. (These claims will be examined more carefully in chapter 11.)

To back the first claim, Boswell explored and produced abundant material on the Middle Ages, arguing that the intolerance of that period toward unpopular minorities (including homosexuals) is what really began the Christian "tradition" of condemning homosexuality. To prove his second claim, he turned to the original language of the specific verses in Genesis, Leviticus, Romans, 1 Corinthians, and 1 Timothy that have been traditionally understood to condemn homosexuality. Here he attempts to prove that each verse has been mistranslated or misunderstood in modern times.

Boswell's tactics were brilliant. Early in his book he dismantles the reader's confidence in his own ability to understand the Bible—an important first step, since anyone reading the Bible cover to cover, without bias, would conclude that it prohibits homosexuality. He then moves on with an enlightening (and thoroughly enjoyable) tour of ancient writings on sexuality, civil law, poetry, and religion, all in an attempt to assure us that early Christian writers were not as concerned about homosexuality as we are today.

Finally he examines the verses mentioned previously, breaking them down in their original language and putting them in historical context. Here Boswell is at his dazzling best. Claiming to understand Moses and Paul's language—thus understanding what they *really* meant to say—he stands traditional beliefs on their heads by turning simple references to homosexuality into descriptions of rape, inhospitality, ritual impurity, or male prostitution. The reader, almost certainly unfamiliar with Greek or Hebrew, is left gaping.

When an author's credentials are impressive and lengthy, and his stature among academics is high, his conclusions may be swallowed whole by the public and the media. This is especially true of "experts" contributing to the homosexual debate. Kinsey's "ten percent of the population is homosexual" myth was accepted and repeated for decades before it was seriously challenged and disproven. Dr. Simon LeVay's 1991 study on the hypothalamus, allegedly proving that homosexuality is genetic, was snapped up by the media and continues to be cited as "proof" that gays are born gay, though LeVay himself denies he ever proved such a thing. And, of course, if the American Psychiatric Association decided that homosexuality is normal, who are we as mere laypeople to disagree?[9]

So it is with Boswell. His credentials were intact, and no one reading his book could deny its scholarly tone. (Indeed, I have been in debates where my gay opponents whipped out their copy of Boswell and confidently pointed to his *credentials* as proof that we should accept his *conclusions*.)[10] But credentials and a scholarly tone do not necessarily yield truth. Before accepting Boswell's conclusions about homosexuality and the Bible, some points about him and his work need to be raised.

First, Boswell was gay.[11] (He died of AIDS in 1994.) That in itself does not disqualify him from writing on the subject, but his own stake in the issue cannot be ignored. He admits as much, perhaps inadvertently, when he opens his book by stating: "No matter how much historians and their readers may wish to avoid contaminating their understanding of the past with the values of the present, they cannot ignore the fact that both writer and reader are inevitably affected by [their] assumptions and beliefs."[12]

Boswell was also, as Professor Elodie Ballantine Emig points out in her excellent series on Boswell and the pro-gay theology, "neither a linguist nor a classicist, but an historian."[13] Historians may write about language, of course, but when they do, it should be remembered that they write as historians, not as experts on language.

Also, though he wrote with genuine respect for the Bible as a document, he had unusual ideas about its purpose. Of the New Testament, for example, he wrote:

> In general, only the most pressing moral questions are addressed by its authors. Details of life appear only to illustrate larger points. No effort is made to elaborate a comprehensive sexual ethic: Jesus and His followers simply responded to situations and questions requiring immediate attention.[14]

Boswell's view makes the Bible look almost acciden-
tal—a good but incomplete book, inadequate to answer
the important questions of life. Compare this to the
apostle Paul's assessment: "All Scripture is given by inspiration of God, and is profitable for doctrine, for reproof, for correction, for instruction in righteousness:
That the man of God may be perfect, thoroughly fur-
nished unto all good works" (2 Timothy 3:16-17).

Boswell's lack of confidence in the Bible's ability, *on
its own,* to provide a "comprehensive sexual ethic" or to
address far-reaching (not just "pressing") concerns,
leaves readers with a convenient loophole: If the Bible
doesn't sufficiently address sexuality, then guidance in
that area must be sought elsewhere. And "elsewhere"
will no doubt include the mental health and sociological
disciplines, both of which take a much friendlier view of
homosexuality than the Bible does.

None of these concerns kept Boswell's book from being widely celebrated upon its release. It was hailed by
literary critics as "groundbreaking," "revolutionary," "as-
tonishing," and it went on to win the 1981 American
Book Award for History. More significantly, it became an
anchor to the gay Christian movement. Finally, their
view had been validated in what many felt were conservative biblical terms. Each verse referring to homosexuality had been explained in its original language and
context, and no fundamentalist Christian could deny
that this was the best way to interpret Scripture. (Chapter 10, though, will look at Boswell's interpretations
more closely.) Moreover, these verses were explained in
what seemed to be airtight arguments, scholarly and
even a bit intimidating in their presentation. No one has
improved on them, though they laid the foundation for
future pro-gay authors Robin Scroggs, Bruce Bowrer,
and the *New Republic's* Andrew Sullivan.

But if Boswell was lauded by gays and journalists,
he was largely ignored by the conservative church. Gay
Christian materials were not likely to find their way into
the libraries of conservative pastors, after all, and they

were seldom if ever reviewed in magazines such as *Christianity Today* and *Moody Monthly*. Indeed, Boswell and the pro-gay theology remained almost unknown to conservatives for nearly a decade.

His arguments began cropping up in debates within mainline denominations, though, forcing conservatives in those circles to analyze and respond to his claims. Only later, as the pro-gay theology emerged in fundamentalist and evangelical discussions, was it taken seriously by those groups. (To my knowledge, in fact, only two conservative authors have devoted an entire book to challenging it; both books came out in 1995, some 14 years after Boswell!)

Today, *Christianity, Social Tolerance and Homosexuality* is still a primary resource for the gay Christian movement.

Homosexuality and the National Council of Churches

Armed with a stronger theological base, the gay Christian movement sought to mainstream itself within the larger Christian community. The most notable effort during the 1980s and early 1990s was the Universal Fellowship of Metropolitan Community Church's attempt to join the National Council of Churches.

On September 9, 1981, the UFMCC applied for membership in the ecumenical National Council of Churches of Christ USA. The amount of controversy raised by a pro-gay denomination joining the NCC can be measured by the NCC's public response upon hearing, through the media, of the UFMCC's intentions. Before the UFMCC even filed, the NCC sent them word, also via the media, that any attempt to join their organization would be "impertinent foolishness."[16]

Undeterred, the UFMCC officially submitted its application. Their intentions, according to Troy Perry, were twofold. First, they sought solidarity with other Christians as they endured antagonism both from conservative believers and gays who felt hostile toward any church, even a gay one. Second, they sought to contribute, to the National Council of Churches, what Perry calls a "new reality": "We offered a broader, more inclusive understanding of sexuality, and the opportunity to reconsider their ideas concerning religion, love, and sex."[17]

Considering the liberal reputation the National Council of Churches already had, Perry and the UFMCC knew the public relations problem they would have if even the NCC rejected them. So they pressed on, viewing their alignment with other denominations as "part of the healing process."[18]

(I've heard this phrase, "the healing process," used many times in connection with the gay Christian movement. More often than not, it is meant both as an acceptance of one's self as being gay and Christian, and as tangible acceptance from other people, especially people not normally sympathetic to the gay cause. Seen in this way, the UFMCC's desire for involvement with the National Council of Churches is understandable.)

For two years, representatives of the Metropolitan Community Church participated in extended discussions with the NCC explaining their views on homosexuality and related subjects. They even conducted an ecumenical service for NCC members in the spring of 1983.

That Fall, the National Council of Churches, after years of deliberations and emotional meetings, decided to table indefinitely any further plans to accept the UFMCC into membership. While this was no doubt a disappointment to the UFMCC, the amount of time the National Council of Churches devoted to examining their membership, and the friends the UFMCC won in the process, was a victory in itself. The struggle to join the NCC showed just how far the gay Christian movement had come, and how far it had yet to go.

Increasing Aggression

As the gay Christian movement continued finding allies in churches and secular circles, it continued to follow the trends of the larger gay rights movement. And the gay rights movement's most noticeable trend, from the mid-1980s into the 1990s, was aggression.

The AIDS epidemic, in full bloom by the mid-80s, fueled a strident form of gay activism. Groups such as the AIDS Coalition to Unleash Power (ACT UP), Queer Nation, and the Lesbian Avengers caught the public's eye as they staged boisterous demonstrations and invaded churches and corporations they considered to be "enemies."

The gay Christian movement did not take long to develop its own style of aggression. Fundamental to its identity were two beliefs: Homosexuality is not unbiblical, and homosexuals can't change, even if they want to.

The reason for the first belief is obvious: The movement could not claim legitimacy if it didn't insist it was biblically legitimate. The necessity for the second belief was less obvious, but crucial.

An unwavering belief among conservative Christians is that homosexuals, like all sinners, need to repent. Having repented of their sin, Christ will enable them by His grace to lead godly lives without indulging in homosexual practices. It was—and is—vital to the gay Christian movement's success that it convince everyone, especially its critics, that homosexuality simply cannot be repented of, any more than skin color or gender can be abandoned.

If the testimonies of the gay Christian movement's members were the only ones the conservative church heard, they would make more progress (perhaps) in convincing the church that their sexual orientation was immutable. To their dismay, however, other testimonies were also being heard from former homosexuals.

Exodus International, a coalition of ministries dedicated to helping people overcome homosexuality, had for almost two decades been proclaiming a message in direct opposition to the gay Christian movement: that homosexuality was a sin, and that Christ could free the homosexual. No message could be more intolerable to the gay Christian movement, and in the mid-1980s they determined it had to be silenced.

In 1989 Reverend Sylvia Pennington, whose career was devoted to assuring gay Christians that their behavior was acceptable to God, released her scorching analysis of the "ex-gay movement" titled *Ex-Gays? There Are None!* By compiling stories of women and men who had tried to change from homosexuals to heterosexuals (through Exodus and similar ministries), Pennington argued that anyone attempting to "go straight" was doomed to failure. Her book, the first published broadside against Exodus ministries, threw down the gauntlet from the gay Christian movement to any Christians who claimed to have overcome homosexuality. Debates between "Christian gays" and "ex-gays" were soon commonplace on talk shows and in print.

The gay Christian movement's aggression found an even wider platform when, in 1993, filmmakers Teodoro Maniaci and Francine Rzenik produced a 90-minute documentary on Exodus International titled *One Nation Under God.* First shown at the 1993 Gay and Lesbian Film Festival, *One Nation* featured interviews with gay Christians who, having tried "ex-gay" ministries, now saw themselves in a position to "expose" them. Most of the film devotes itself to their criticisms, attempting to prove, by sheer weight of testimony and emotion, that no homosexual can ever be anything else. In 1994 PBS deemed the film worthy of national exposure on its "Point of View" series. For the first time, all of America was exposed to the arguments from gay Christians as they scoffed at the idea of anyone changing, even through Christ, their sexual orientation.

That same year, Mel White shocked both Christian and secular communities with his revelation of being gay and Christian. Reverend White, already a widely recognized Christian author and filmmaker, released *Stranger at the Gate*, an autobiographical account of his attempts to overcome homosexuality while employed as a ghostwriter by the likes of Jerry Falwell, Billy Graham, and Oliver North.

Never had the gay Christian movement acquired a spokesman with conservative credentials as impressive as Mel White's. His former association with what he now derides as the "Religious Right" adds to his credibility when he attacks his former employers for their "homophobia." And if he—a former pastor, seminarian, and associate of some of the country's most influential Christian leaders—was unable to overcome his homosexuality after years of effort and psychotherapy, how (the gay Christian movement asks) can anyone else be expected to overcome theirs?

Mel White's two primary messages are made clear both in his book and his public appearances: The Religious Right is homophobic and must be stopped, and anyone promoting the idea that homosexuality can be overcome must be silenced.

White's stature—both former and present, as Dean of the country's largest gay church—gives him access to today's top media figures, and he uses it generously. Virtually every major talk and news program has extended a welcome to him, making him the gay Christian movement's most visible and influential representative.

Coming of Age

The gay rights movement's coming of age can be seen in its progressive demands, demands that have evolved, in content and insistence, over the decades:

1. "We're human beings; treat us fairly" (1950–1969).

2. "We're normal and just as good as anyone else" (1969–1979).

3. "We won't tolerate any public opposition to our viewpoint" (1979–present).

As always, the gay Christian movement's messages follow suit:

1. "God loves us too" (1969–1976).

2. "Not only does God love us, but He also approves of our being gay" (1976–1979).

3. "Anyone saying we can't be gay *and* Christian must be stopped" (1980–present).

By now, we've reviewed the events leading to the expansion of the gay Christian movement, and how the church has responded to it. It will be useful, now, to examine the pro-gay theology itself, and to understand how and why people come to accept it.

6

The Pro-Gay
Theology

*"For this cause God shall send them strong
delusion, that they should believe a lie"*
— 2 Thessalonians 2:11

By now the reader should have a general understanding of how both the gay rights and gay Christian movements came about. The larger questions need to be asked now: Exactly *what* does the gay Christian movement believe, and *how* did the advocates of the movement come to believe it?

In the chapters that follow I will seek to more fully answer the first question—which, frankly, will be much easier than answering the second. Explaining *what* a group believes is not hard. Explaining *how* they came to believe it is another matter.

We can't read people's minds or motives. That, I am sure, is one reason Jesus warned us against judging others (Matthew 7:1). Unless we are given divine insight into another's motives (as Peter was given in Acts 8:20-23), we can't say for certain why people embrace false teachings. We *can* be certain the teachings themselves are false; *why* people have accepted them is something we can't prove one way or another.

Yet the Bible offers us some clues on this issue. And testimonies from members of the gay Christian movement are also enlightening. Both of these will be considered in this chapter as we try to understand what the gay Christian movement believes, and what personal and spiritual factors may have influenced those who hold to these beliefs.

The Pro-Gay Theology in Brief

The pro-gay theology is the cornerstone of the gay Christian movement, just as the Athanasian and Nicene Creeds are the foundation of most Protestant beliefs.[1] The movement is diverse; some of its spokespersons such as Robert Williams, Bishop Spong, and Jane Spahr promote flamboyant and blatantly heretical ideas. But most groups within the gay Christian movement ostensibly subscribe to traditional theology. (The "Statement of Faith" of the UFMCC, for example, is based on the Apostles' and Nicene Creeds.)[2]

Discuss basic Christianity with a member of the gay Christian movement and you will be in agreement on many points: the Godhead, the work of Christ, the inerrancy of the Bible, the final judgment, and so forth. This is one reason the pro-gay theology is so seductive. Like many errors, it contains major portions of truth.

Yet in conversations with gay spokesmen, both as one who formerly supported the gay Christian movement and, now, as one who opposes it, I have noticed departures from sound doctrine that keep arising. The first has to do with biblical authority. Gay Christian leaders are quick to say they believe in it, but at times their definition of what it is can be disturbing.

Troy Perry's assertion that "scientific information, social changes, and personal experience are the greatest forces for change in the way we interpret the Bible" is unsettling.[3] Social change and personal experiences are irrelevant to truth; Jesus Christ, who is the same yesterday, today, and forever (Hebrews 13:8), is not known to follow social trends. Boswell's remarks about the inadequacy of Scripture to answer life's problems (also mentioned earlier) betray ambiguity about biblical authority as well.

I have found this ambiguity to be fairly common. During a radio debate with a UFMCC minister, when asked how he discerned God's truth, he said there were three sources he relied on, each having equal authority: the Bible, the witness of his own heart, and the witness of his community. I responded that I had no such confidence in either my heart or my community—the Bible was the ultimate authority in all matters.

In another discussion at a Presbyterian church in Washington DC, I was challenged by the local representative of the Presbyterian Lesbian and Gay Concerns Committee: "You keep talking about the Bible. I want to know what you think about the Holy Spirit!" I think the Holy Spirit is wonderful, and I said as much. But I also said that when it came to matters of doctrine, I could not trust my ability to discern the Spirit's voice. That, I argued, was exactly why God gave us a written standard (which was inspired by the Spirit): so we need not guess at what He wills.

My opponent disagreed; and there, I'm sure, was our main difference. He felt that matters such as sexuality could be decided by what one subjectively thinks the Spirit is saying to the individual; I contend that we have to objectively rely on the written Word alone.

Another serious problem the gay Christian movement faces has to do with sexual ethics. The church has clear guidelines for sexual behavior: Intercourse before marriage is forbidden, marriage must be monogamous, and divorce is permissible only in the event of fornication or abandonment by an unbelieving spouse.

During my involvement with the gay church, we made virtually no effort to abide by these standards. Among gay men (religious or not) it was unheard of to wait until a marriage (or "union ceremony," as it was called then) before engaging in sex. Indeed, sexual rela-

tions within days or even hours of meeting were not uncommon, and they were never, in my experience, criti-
cized from the pulpit.

Monogamy, though usually held up as an ideal, was
seldom (to my knowledge) adhered to. And the dissolu-
tion of a relationship required far less than abandonment or adultery. Most couples I knew broke up because
of incompatibility, or one partner's interest in a third
party.

Of course, problems such as these are common in all
churches, but most churches at least hold to a standard
of chastity before marriage and monogamy during it.
Though things may have changed since the onset of the
AIDS epidemic, I saw no such standards being consistently upheld in the gay Christian movement.

Still, the movement claims a conservative theological
base, and in most gay churches, I found that to be true.
But some additions were made to the basic tenants of
the faith—additions vital to the pro-gay theology.

First, homosexuality is viewed as being God-ordained. As such, it is viewed as being on a par with heterosexuality. Mel White points out, quite accurately,
that "if you don't see that premise [that God created ho-
mosexuality] then gay marriage looks ridiculous, if not
insane."[4]

But to be seen as created by God, the traditional understanding of homosexuality must be discredited. This
is done in four basic ways within the gay Christian
movement.

First, prejudice against homosexuals is blamed for
the understanding most Christians have of the biblical
references to it. John Boswell emphasizes this point
throughout *Christianity, Social Tolerance and Homosexuality.* Troy Perry repeats this point early in his book as
well: "To condemn homosexuals, many denominations
have intentionally misread and misinterpreted their
Bibles to please their own personal preferences."[5] So,
according to Perry and others, not only are most Christians wrong about homosexuality, but many or most are

intentionally wrong, deliberately reading their prejudice against gays into the Bible.

Mel White goes even further, stating that major leaders in the Christian community—Jerry Falwell, James Kennedy, and Pat Robertson—take public stands against the gay rights movement for the sake of raising funds and increasing their visibility.[6] Casting doubt on the motives of conservative leaders, and numerous denominations, makes it easier to discount their Bible-based objections to homosexuality. No wonder this tactic is so common in the gay Christian movement.

Others within the movement contend that the Scriptures we understand to condemn homosexuality have actually been mistranslated. Wainwright Churchill and Roger Biery insist on this; Boswell, of course, expounds on it considerably. Thus, according to this view, the Bible should be taken literally *in its original language*; the problem with most Christians, they say, is that they do not know biblical Greek and Hebrew well enough to realize that our modern translations on homosexuality are all wrong.

Another claim that pro-gay theorists make is that the verses that seem to prohibit homosexuality (Leviticus 18:22; 20:13; Romans 1:26-27; 1 Corinthians 6:9-10; 1 Timothy 1:9-10) have actually been yanked out of context from their original meaning. Or, as Boswell, Perry, and Scroogs point out, they only applied to the culture existing at the time they were written. (Scroogs, for example, claims that "biblical judgments about homosexuality are not relevant to today's debate."[7])

These arguments do not sit well with most Bible-believing Christians. The Scriptures mentioned above are so clear and specific that they defy misinterpretation of any sort. "Thou shalt not lie with a man as with a woman" is just as clear as "Thou shalt not kill." It is intellectually dishonest to say that conservatives "interpret" such verses out of prejudice against homosexuals. Those same "prejudiced" conservatives (Falwell, Kennedy, Robertson, and others) also take Scriptures against heterosexual sins quite literally. If they only prohibit homosexuality out of their own prejudice, why on earth do they, as heterosexuals, also condemn heterosexual sins? The argument makes no sense.

Neither does the "mistranslation" argument make sense. We can allow some discrepancy in minor areas of translation. On something as important as sexual ethics, however, are we really to believe that the Bible translators we rely on got it wrong five different times, in two different Testaments? And *only* on the Scriptures regarding homosexuality? (Pro-gay apologists seem to have no problem with the other Scriptures condemning sins such as adultery and child abuse.)

Equally hard to swallow is the "out of context" argument. The fact is, in Leviticus, Romans, 1 Corinthians, and 1 Timothy, homosexuality is mentioned *in the context of sexual and immoral behavior!* The context is quite clear—a variety of behaviors are prohibited; homosexuality, along with adultery, fornication, and idolatry, is one of them.

The "cultural" argument fares no better. In some cases, a Scripture may seem culturally bound. (Examples include injunctions against long hair on men, or women speaking to their husbands during church.) But again—*five times*? Five different Scriptures, from both Testaments, addressed to highly different cultures (including the Hebrew and the Roman) are obviously not culturally bound. The cultures these verses are addressed to are just too different.

All of this leaves conservatives highly skeptical of the gay Christian movement's claim to respect biblical authority. It takes mental gymnastics to accept these arguments, and those not having a stake in accepting them are unlikely to do so.

But those who have a personal interest in the pro-gay theology are another matter. Deciding to believe what you *want* to believe (as I did) is the first step. The next is to make the Bible agree with you. That's nothing new; people have been doing it for years.

Twenty years ago, for example, I was informed by a rather libertarian Christian that smoking marijuana was permissible and, in fact, biblical.

"Where did you get a notion like that?" I gasped.

"From Genesis 1:29," he said, confidently turning to the Old Testament. "Right here, see?" His finger rested on the verse: "And God said, Behold, I have given you every herb bearing seed."

No, he wasn't kidding. Neither was the Christian couple I once knew who justified their passion for nude beaches by reminding me of Adam and Eve's original state. "Ought we not to be as they were?" they asked innocently. "Naked and unashamed?"

Twist the Scriptures hard enough and you can make them appear to say anything you please. It's not that hard to do. I remember, having already decided to express myself homosexually, how I read the Bible through the eyes of my decision, rather than objectively. Paul Morris raises this very issue when he warns: "But if I were a Christian homosexual, I think this one question would disturb me most: Am I trying to interpret Scripture in the light of my proclivity; or should I interpret my proclivity in the light of Scripture?"[8]

An unfortunate pattern of doing the former can be seen in the gay Christian movement's testimonials. Troy Perry writes about having already decided that homosexuality was acceptable, and *then* searching the Bible to equip himself to answer conservatives.[9] In his book Mel White alludes to some earlier studies of the destruction of Sodom,[10] but his turning point seems to have come not from a careful, prayerful study of Scripture, but from a psychologist who encouraged him to accept his homosexuality and find a lover![11]

Musician Marsha Stevens gives a lengthy account of her acceptance of lesbianism without once explaining how she reached the point of believing that homosexuality was scripturally acceptable. (The closest she comes is in telling how she prayed one night for confirmation that lesbianism was okay; the next morning someone gave her a pin saying, "Born Again Lesbian."[12]) For someone spiritually raised under the teachings of Chuck Smith, who always emphasizes the Word of God over experience, that is astounding.

Or maybe it isn't. A sign of the end times, according to the apostle Paul, will be an abandonment of truth for the sake of personal fulfillment:

> In the last days perilous times shall come. For men shall be lovers of their own selves (2 Timothy 3:1-2).

> For the time will come when they will not endure sound doctrine; but after their own lusts shall they heap to themselves teachers, having itching ears and they shall turn away their ears from the truth (2 Timothy 4:3-4).

Self over truth, man over God—can a Christian be so deceived? Evidently so, for Paul referred to the Galatian church as having been "bewitched" (Galatians 3:1), and Jesus warned that a prominent sign of the days before His coming would be an increase in deception (Matthew 24:4). To confront the pro-gay theology, then, is to confront a deceptive element of our time—the tendency to subjugate objective truth to subjective experience.

That's one reason confrontation is not enough to change a heart. Being knowledgeable enough to dismantle all the gay Christian movement's claims won't be enough to persuade a homosexual to repent. The heart, having been hardened through deception or rebellion or both, has to be softened. And that is the work of God alone. Ours is to simply speak the truth, trusting Him to quicken it to our hearers. With that in mind, having grasped a general understanding of pro-gay theological beliefs, let's move on to a point-by-point description of its claims, and a rebuttal to each.

The arguments I will present against homosexuality in chapters 7 through 11, by the way, are based on my belief in the authority of the Bible. They are different from arguments based on reason or science, which might be better applied when arguing to nonreligious homosexuals. But to those in the gay Christian movement, since they claim to believe in the inspiration of Scripture, we can appeal to the Bible as the final authority. Thus the arguments I've presented are unapologetically biblical.

May God help us to speak the truth in love as we confront the pro-gay theology.

7

SOCIAL JUSTICE ARGUMENTS— PART ONE

The Nature of Homosexuality

"I firmly believe that we cannot tolerate discrimination against any individuals or groups in our country. I appreciate so much your encouraging me to help change attitudes."

— Former First Lady Barbara Bush, 1990 letter to the Parents and Friends of Lesbians and Gays (PFLAG)

Bigotry makes us queasy. It reminds us of man's dark side, documented in photos from Nazi Germany and history books describing slavery in America. We recoil from it, partly out of disgust and partly, I believe, out of collective guilt. We are ashamed to recall our country's institutionalized racism; we're all too aware that the disease still thrives, both here and abroad. So when charges of discrimination are thrown around, we duck. The last thing we want to be accused of is bigotry.

This puts us in a bind when charges of bigotry against homosexuals are leveled against us. We have heard of people protesting gay parades, waving signs

saying "God Hates Fags," and similar nonsense; naturally, we distance ourselves from them. But in doing so,
we risk being silent altogether on the subject of homosexuality, for fear of being lumped into the "extremist"
category.

That is exactly what pro-gay strategists are hoping
for. Homosexual authors Marshall Kirk and Hunter
Madsen, offering ideas for furthering gay rights, blatantly
admit the power of "guilt-tripping" the heterosexual population:

> The purpose of [gay] victim imagery is to make
> straights [heterosexuals] feel very uncomfort-
> able—gays should be portrayed as victims of
> prejudice. Straights must be shown graphic
> pictures of brutalized gays, dramatizations of
> job and housing insecurities, loss of child cus-
> tody, public humiliation, etc.[1]

No decent person can be indifferent to victims of
prejudice. And when gays are seen as "brutalized," who
wants to criticize their behavior? That alone can intimi-
date us into compromising our stand on homosexuality—
or taking no stand at all.

That is the power of "social justice arguments." They
call for fair treatment and recognition of past injustices,
along with assurances that those injustices will not be
repeated. They also put anyone who disagrees with the
"victims" on the defensive, discrediting their arguments
and painting them in the worst possible light.

Social justice arguments are also effective because
they sound so good. They demand an end to homophobia and insensitivity; who wants to say that they're
against such goals? But just as the question "When
did you stop beating your wife, Mr. Jones?" assumes
(without proof) that Mr. Jones *has* been beating her, so
the pro-gay social justice arguments assume (without
proof) that gays are victims, and that the conservative
church is largely responsible for their victimhood.

These arguments are most effective in secular discussions—talk shows, interviews, university debates—where listeners are unlikely to judge them by biblical standards. Instead of discerning what side is theologically correct, non-Christian audiences tend to side with whoever seems "nicest." Usually, that means the gay spokesman asking for antidiscrimination laws or support clubs for gay teenagers. The person against these things—usually a conservative Christian—doesn't seem "nice," no matter how nice he may truly be.

That is not to say that pro-gay social justice arguments are unwinnable; answered properly and politely, unbiblical ideas can be challenged in the secular arena. Paul proved that with the citizens at Mars Hill (Acts 17:22). But the Christian challenger needs to be aware that often, because of his position, he willl be seen as the bad guy. And that is all the more reason to speak with an equal measure of clarity and politeness.

Thomas Schmidt, in his excellent critique of the pro-gay theology, minces no words on this point: "Christians who cannot yet deal with the issues [pertaining to homosexuality] calmly and compassionately should keep their mouths shut, and they should certainly stay away from the front lines of ministry and public policy debate—not to mention television talk shows."[2]

Arguments based on the *nature* of homosexuality attempt to prove it is inborn, unchangeable, normal, and common; therefore, it should be accepted as equal to heterosexuality. To challenge such arguments, the challenger must dismantle pro-gay assumptions (gays are victims; conservative Christians and their beliefs are persecutors) by pointing out when and how those assumptions are either *illogical, misleading,* or *exaggerated.* We will look for at least one of those three elements when responding to pro-gay arguments.

In this chapter we will examine social justice arguments based on the nature of homosexuality itself. Arguments based on society's response to homosexuals will be reviewed in chapter 8.

Social Justice Arguments Based on the Nature of Homosexuality

General Argument One: Homosexuality is inborn.

As the gay rights movement has evolved, the notion of homosexuality being something that one is born with—like gender or hair color—has gained wide approval, especially among gays themselves. In the 1940s, when sexologist Alfred Kinsey asked homosexuals how they "got that way," only nine percent claimed to have been born gay.[3] In 1970, nearly the same percentage of 979 gays in San Francisco answered the same way.[4] But 13 years later, when the gay rights movement had become more politicized, 35 percent of 147 homosexuals said they were born that way.[5] And today, most gay leaders, especially in the gay Christian movement, would agree with Mel White's assertion that homosexuality is "a gift from God to be embraced, celebrated, lived with integrity."[6] The "inborn theory" takes on special significance when viewed religiously. It implies that if something is inborn, God must have created it. And who are we to argue with the Creator?

No doubt many homosexuals sincerely believe they were genetically determined to be gay. But the emergence and growth of that belief, along with the emergence and growth of the gay rights movement, cannot be a coincidence. It is politically expedient to view sexual orientation as inborn; many people who would otherwise consider homosexuality immoral will support gay rights if they can be convinced it is an inherited trait.

William Cheshire, the editorial page editor for the *Arizona Republic*, is a good example. "My feelings about gays and lesbians were dominated by religious beliefs," he said in a 1993 interview with *U.S. News and World Report*. But after reviewing certain studies purporting to prove that homosexuals were born that way, he "did a complete reversal in [his] attitude toward gays and lesbians," and he began actively promoting, through his paper, antidiscrimination laws for gays.[7]

Those in the gay Christian movement may find extra reassurance in studies alleging to prove that their sexual preference is inborn. "I felt in my heart that this [homosexuality] is something I was born with," one gay man enthused. The "born gay" studies, he added, "made me feel good about myself. They made me feel less a sinner."[8]

People tend to view homosexuality more favorably when they think it is inborn. No wonder gay leaders (not all, but most) push the born gay theory; it furthers the cause. (But it's an uphill push—a 1993 survey found that only 32 percent of Americans believe homosexuality is inborn.[9])

Responses to the born gay argument should concentrate on two facts:

1. To date, homosexuality has still not been proven to be genetic or biological in origin.

2. Even if someday it is proven to be inborn, that will not make it normal or morally desirable.

Sub-Argument One: *Homosexuality is inborn. In 1991 Dr. Simon LeVay proved homosexuality to be a result of structures in the hypothalamus. It should therefore be accepted as normal.*

In 1991 Dr. LeVay, a neuroscientist at the Salk Institute of La Jolla, California, examined the brains of 41 cadavers—19 allegedly homosexual men, 16 allegedly heterosexual men, and six allegedly heterosexual women. His study focused on a group of neurons in the hypothalamus structure called the interstitial nuclei of the anterior hypothalamus, or the INAH3.

He reported this region of the brain to be larger in heterosexual men than in homosexuals; likewise, he found it to be larger in heterosexual men than in the women he studied. For that reason, he postulated homosexuality to be inborn, the result of size variations in the INAH3, and his findings were published in *Science* magazine in August 1991.[10] This is the study most often quoted when people insist that homosexuality has been "proven" to be inborn.

Response: This argument is exaggerated and misleading for six reasons:

First, LeVay did not prove homosexuality to be inborn; his results were not uniformly consistent. On the surface it appears that *all* of LeVay's homosexual subjects had smaller INAH3s than his heterosexual ones; in fact, three of the homosexual subjects actually had *larger* INAH3s than the heterosexuals. Additionally, three of the heterosexual subjects had *smaller* INAH3s than the average homosexual subject. Thus, as Dr. John Ankerberg of the Ankerberg Theological Research Institute notes, six of LeVay's 35 male subjects—17 percent of his total study group—contradicted his own theory.[11]

Second, LeVay did not necessarily measure the INAH3 properly. The area LeVay was measuring is quite small—smaller than snowflakes, according to scientists interviewed when his study was released. His peers in the neuroscientific community cannot agree on whether the INAH3 should be measured by its size and volume or by its number of neurons.[12]

Third, it is unclear whether brain structure affects behavior or behavior affects brain structure. Dr. Kenneth Klivington, also of SALK Institute, points out that neurons can change in response to experience. "You could postulate," he says, "that brain change occurs throughout life, as a consequence of experience."[13] In other words, even if there is a significant difference between the brain structures of heterosexual and homosexual men, it is unclear whether the brain structure caused homosexuality, or if homosexuality affected brain structure.

In fact, one year after LeVay's study was released, Dr. Lewis Baxter of UCLA obtained evidence that behavioral therapy can produce changes in brain circuitry, reinforcing the idea that behavior can and does affect brain structure.[14] So even if differences *do* exist between the

INAH3s of homosexual and heterosexual men, it is possible that the diminished size of the homosexual's is caused by his behavior, rather than his behavior being caused by the INAH3's size.

Fourth, LeVay was not certain which of his subjects were homosexual and which were heterosexual. He admits this represents a "distinct shortcoming" in his study. Having only case histories on his subjects to go by (which were by no means guaranteed to provide accurate information about the patient's sexual orientation), he could only assume that, if a patient's records did *not* indicate he was gay, he must have been heterosexual.

Yet six of the 16 reportedly heterosexual men studied had died of AIDS, increasing the chances that their sexual histories may have been incompletely recorded.[15] If it is uncertain which of LeVay's subjects were heterosexual and which were homosexual, how useful can his conclusions about "differences" between them really be?

Fifth, LeVay did not approach the subject objectively. LeVay, who is openly homosexual, told *Newsweek* magazine that, after the death of his lover, he was determined to find a genetic cause for homosexuality or he would abandon science altogether. Furthermore, he admitted that he hoped to educate society about homosexuality, affecting legal and religious attitudes toward it.[16] None of this diminishes his credentials as a neuroscientist. But his research can hardly be said to have been unbiased.

Sixth, the scientific community did not by any means unanimously accept LeVay's study. Comments from other scientists in response to LeVay's work are noteworthy. Dr. Richard Nakamura of the National Institute of Mental Health says it will take a "larger effort to be convinced there is a link between this structure and homosexuality."[17] Dr. Anne Fausto-Sterling of Brown University is less gentle in her response: "My freshman biology students know enough to sink this study."[18]

Dr. Rochelle Kliner, a psychiatrist at Medical College of Virginia, doubts we will "ever find a single cause of homosexuality."[19] *Scientific American* sums up the reason many professionals approach the INAH3 theory with caution: "LeVay's study has yet to be fully replicated by another researcher."[20]

Sub-Argument Two: *Homosexuality is inborn. A study of men with homosexual twins found that twin brothers of gay men are more likely to be homosexual than heterosexual.*

In 1991 psychologist Michael Bailey of Northwestern University (a gay rights advocate) and psychiatrist Richard Pillard of Boston University School of Medicine (who is openly homosexual) compared sets of identical male twins to fraternal twins (whose genetic ties are less close). In each set, at least one twin was homosexual. They found that, among the identical twins, 52 percent were both homosexual, as opposed to the fraternal twins, among whom only 22 percent shared a homosexual orientation.[21] Pillard and Bailey suggested that the higher incidence of shared homosexuality among identical twins meant that homosexuality was genetic in origin.

Response: This argument is misleading and exaggerated for four reasons:

First, Pillard and Bailey's findings actually indicate that something besides genes must account for homosexuality. If 48 percent of identical twins, who are closely linked genetically, do *not* share the same sexual orientation, then genetics alone *cannot* account for homosexuality. Bailey admitted as much by stating, "There must be something in the environment to yield the discordant twins."[22]

Second, all the twins Pillard and Bailey studied were raised in the same household. If the sets of twins in which both brothers were homosexual were raised in *separate* homes, it might be easier to believe that genes played a role in their sexual development. But since they were all raised in the same households, it is impossible to know what effect environment played, and what effect, if any, genes played. Dr. Fausto-Sterling commented that "in order for such a study to be at all meaningful, you'd have to look at twins raised apart."[23]

Third, Drs. Pillard and Bailey, like Dr. LeVay, did not approach their subject objectively. Their personal feelings about homosexuality, like LeVay's, certainly do not disqualify them from doing good research on the subject. But their feelings must be, at the very least, considered. Pillard said, in fact, "A genetic component in sexual orientation says, 'This is not a fault,'" and both he and Bailey stated that they hoped their work would "disprove homophobic claims."[24]

Fourth, a later study on twins yielded results different from Pillard and Bailey's. In March 1992 the *British Journal of Psychiatry* published a report on homosexuals who are twins (both fraternal and identical) and found that only 20 percent of the homosexual twins had a gay co-twin, leading the researchers to conclude that "genetic factors are insufficient explanation of the development of sexual orientation."[25] Not only has Pillard and Bailey's work not been replicated; when a similar study was conducted, it got completely different results.

Sub-Argument Three: *Homosexuality is inborn. It has been linked to a gene on the X chromosome, which is inherited from the mother.*

In 1993 Dr. Dean Hamer of the National Cancer Institute studied 40 pairs of non-identical gay brothers and claimed that 33 of the pairs had inherited the same X-linked genetic markers. This allegedly indicates a genetic cause for homosexuality.[26]

Response One: This argument is misleading and exaggerated for two reasons.

First, like LeVay's study, Hamer's results have yet to be replicated. Again, it should be noted that a lack of replication does *not* mean a study is invalid; it only means that the study's conclusions have not been confirmed by further research.

Second, a later, similar study actually contradicted Hamer's conclusions. George Ebers of the University of Western Ontario examined 52 pairs of gay brothers, and found "no evidence for a linkage of homosexuality to markers on the X-chromosome or elsewhere."[27] Ebers with an associate, also studied 400 families with one or more homosexual males, and found "no evidence for the X-linked, mother-to-son transmission posited by Hamer."[28]

Response Two: This argument, like those based on LeVay, Pillard, and Bailey's work, is illogical in that it assumes "inborn" means "normal" or "morally acceptable." This assumption is faulty for three reasons:

First, "inborn" and "normal" are not necessarily the same. Even if homosexuality is someday proven to be inborn, *inborn* does not necessarily mean *normal.* Any number of defects or handicaps, for example, may be inborn, but we would hardly call them normal for that reason alone. Why should we be compelled to call homosexuality normal, just because it may be inborn?

Second, inborn tendencies toward certain behaviors (such as homosexuality) do not make those behaviors moral. Studies in the past 15 years indicate that a variety of behaviors may have their roots in genetics or biology. In 1983 the former director of the National Council on Alcoholism reported on a number of chemical events that can produce alcoholism.[29] In 1991, the City of Hope Medical Center found a certain gene present in 77 percent of their alcoholic patients.[30] Obesity and violent behavior are now thought to be genetically influenced.[31] Even infidelity, according to research reported in *Time* magazine, may be in our genes![32]

Surely we are not going to say that obesity, violence, alcoholism, and adultery are legitimate because they were inherited. So it is with homosexuality. Whether inborn or acquired, it is still, like all sexual contact apart from marriage, *immoral.* And immoral behavior cannot be legitimized by a quick baptism in the gene pool.

Third, we are a fallen race, born in sin. Scripture teaches that we inherited a corrupt sin nature that affects us physically and spiritually (Psalm 51:5; Romans 5:12). We were born spiritually dead (John 3:5-6) and physically imperfect (1 Corinthians 15:1-54). We cannot assume, then, that because something is inborn, it is also God-ordained. There are mental, psychological, physical, and sexual aspects of our beings that God never intended us to have. Inborn, in short, does not mean "divinely sanctioned."

Response Three: Professional researchers are by no means unanimously convinced of the "homosexuality is inborn" argument.

Some researchers, according to the *Chronicle of Higher Education,* actually say the "born gay" theories are "unfounded and politically dangerous."[33] Dr. William Byne of Columbia University calls the inborn evidence "inconclusive," and compares it to "trying to add up a hundred zeroes so you can get one."[34] Dr. Fausto-Sterling says the studies, and ensuing debate, are not even about biology but about politics.[35] Professor John D'Emilio of the University of North Carolina, while willing to consider the possibility of inborn homosexuality, says there is "too much else we haven't explored."[36]

General Argument Two: Homosexuals cannot be changed.

"Sexual orientation simply cannot be changed," a gay psychiatrist says confidently,[37] warning that "there may be severe emotional and social consequences in the attempt to change from homosexuality to heterosexuality."[38]

This argument draws heavily from the social sciences, as it must; the Bible supports no such claim.

Indeed, the apostle Paul makes the opposite remark, clearly stating that homosexuals *can* change, when he asserts: "Neither fornicators, nor idolators, nor adulterers, nor effeminate, nor homosexuals . . . will inherit the kingdom of God. And such *were* some of you, but you were washed, but you were sanctified, but you are justified in the name of the Lord Jesus" (1 Corinthians 6:9-10, NKJV, emphasis added).

Of course, the gay Christian apologist does not believe this verse refers to homosexuality, which brings us to the crux of the issue—whether or not homosexual behavior is, according to the Bible, *a sin.* If it is, there's no argument over whether or not it can be changed. Christ frees us from the power of sin (Romans 6:14) as we become new creatures in Him (2 Corinthians 5:17). By this we are certain that any sin condemned in Scripture can be overcome by God's grace.

But if the gay apologists really believe that homosexuality is *not* a biblically forbidden sin, why do they bother arguing, vehemently, that they cannot change? If something is not a sin, after all, then it doesn't matter if it's inborn or chosen, immutable or changeable.

Allow me to make a frivolous comparison. I believe it was all right, in God's sight, for me to marry an Italian woman. I have always thought olive-skinned, dark-haired women are particularly beautiful, and I think that's perfectly okay. I don't care whether my taste for dark hair and olive complexions is inborn or acquired, nor do I see any need to prove that it's "unchangeable." Maybe it is, maybe it isn't—but since I feel good about it, who cares?

Now, if someone came along and told me that the Bible condemned my attraction to dark hair, I would ask them to show me where the Bible condemned it. If I was convinced that their biblical interpretation was wrong—as I'm sure I would be—then I woud leave it at that. I certainly wouldn't bother explaining psychological or biological roots that may have influenced my attractions.

If I felt right about them before God, they would need no explanation.

Which begs the question: *Aren't gay Christian spokesmen betraying a certain self-doubt when they try so hard to prove their sexuality is inborn and unchangeable?*

At any rate, the unchangeable argument plays a major role in gay Christian thinking. Mel White repeats it throughout his book; his former wife, in fact, takes it on herself to speak for all homosexuals when she says, "After all those decades of trying, we discovered that no one can choose or change his or her sexual orientation."[39]

Troy Perry is just as adamant: "There is no 'cure' (for homosexuality). Those who make claims to the contrary are charlatans, or are inadequately informed persons who for any of many possible reasons try to delude themselves or their associates."[40]

Scanzoni and Mollenkott refer to Christians who "believe" they have been cured from homosexuality.[41] Pennington scoffs at the very notion of "ex-gay."[42]

One former homosexual, quoted in Thomas Schmidt's book, makes a point I've always suspected when he explains why many gays feel so strongly about the change issue: "Homosexual activists want to convince not only the public, but *themselves* that change never occurs, because *if I exist, each of them must be haunted by the possibility that they, too, might find the power to change.*"[43]

But if they insist there is no such power, and rely on clinical authorities to support their position, then that position can be answered by *other* clinical authorities who insist that homosexuality *is* changeable. (In chapter 9 we will return to the "change" issue and address it from a more theological perspective.)

Response One: The "unchangeable" argument is misleading. While many mental health authorities believe homosexuality is unchangeable, many others believe it *can* be changed.

In 1970 the Kinsey Institute reported that 84 percent of the homosexuals they studied had shifted their sexual orientation at least once; 32 percent of them reported a second shift; and 13 percent reported *five changes*, during their lifetime, in their sexual orientation![44]

The director of the New York Center for Psychoanalytic Training, no doubt aware that such changes occur, remarked on the "misinformation spread by certain circles that homosexuality is untreatable," saying it did "incalculable harm to thousands."[45]

Dr. Irvine Bieber concluded, after treating more than 100 homosexuals, that "a heterosexual shift is a possibility for all homosexuals who are strongly motivated to change."[46]

Sex researchers Masters and Johnson (hardly a pair of standard-bearers for conservative virtues!) said that the "homosexuality cannot be changed" concept was "certainly open to question."[47] Drs. Wood and Dietrich, writing about the effectiveness of treatment for homosexuality, confirmed that "all studies which have attempted conversions from homosexuality to heterosexuality have had significant success."[48] And the "New Report of the Kinsey Institute" explains that people do not "necessarily maintain the same sexual orientation throughout their lives," and then explains that "programs helping homosexuals change report varying degrees of success."[49]

But no one says it better than Stanton Jones, Chair of Psychology at Wheaton College: "Anyone who says there is no hope [for change] is either ignorant or a liar. Every secular study of change has shown some success rate, and persons who testify to substantial healings by God are legion."[50]

Response Two: This argument is illogical in that it assumes that if a condition is unchangeable it is therefore desirable.

For the sake of argument, suppose it *could* be proven that homosexuality, as a condition, is unchangeable— that no amount of prayer, counseling, or efforts of any sort could make a homosexual become attracted to the opposite sex. *What then?* Should that change our view of homosexual behavior as being sinful?

Hardly. There is no contingency factor in any scriptural reference to any kind of sin, in either the Old or the New Testament. We never read anything like: "Thou shalt not do thus and so!" ("Unless, of course, you tried hard to change, went for prayer and counseling, and found you just couldn't stop wanting to do thus and so. If that's the case, then thus and so is no longer a sin. It's an inborn, immutable gift and you can darn well indulge in it!")

The apostle Paul's thorn in the flesh, whatever it may have been, was unchangeable. Despite his prayers for deliverance, God allowed it to remain. But it certainly was not desirable (2 Corinthians 12:7-9). Other conditions—alcoholism, for example, or various addictions—are widely believed to be unchangeable, and have to be coped with daily. That hardly makes them desirable, natural, or God-ordained.

General Argument Three: Homosexuality is not a mental illness; therefore the church should not condemn it.

This argument draws its strength from the American Psychiatric Association's 1973 decision to delete homosexuality from its list of disorders. (The APA Board of Trustees determines what conditions are listed in the *Diagnostic and Statistical Manual,* which is the official list of mental and emotional disturbances used by all mental health professionals. Obviously, their definition of "normal" has tremendous impact on American life.)

During discussions on homosexuality, the APA's decision to "normalize" it is often referred to as the bottom line. "If the APA decided homosexuality is normal, then it's normal!" is a common remark.

But saying the APA decided one day to normalize homosexuality is a bit like saying General Lee decided one day to meet with General Grant to negotiate. A long, bloody war was fought before the decision was reached; to ignore that is to misrepresent history.

A war was likewise fought within the APA before its landmark decision was reached. The details have been recorded by Ronald Bayer in *Homosexuality and American Psychiatry: The Politics of Diagnosis*. The story has been retold several times, most notably by Kenneth Lewes and William Dannemeyer.

For purposes of this discussion, I will cite the main points of Bayer's description:

1. The American Psychiatric Association had traditionally viewed homosexuality as a disorder prior to 1973. The *Diagnostic and Statistical Manual* (the APA's official list of disorders originally compiled in 1952) listed homosexuality as a sociopathic personality disturbance in its first version.[51] The second version—DSM II—moved homosexuality from the category of personality disturbances to that of sexual deviations in 1968.[52]

2. Gay leaders began protesting the annual conventions of the American Psychiatric Association, demanding a reconsideration of homosexuality's diagnostic status, and further demanding that they be included in any future discussions within the APA on the subject.[53] The APA consented; intense discussion and debate followed.

3. On December 15, 1973, the Board of Trustees of the APA, concluding months of negotiations with gay activists, voted to delete homosexuality altogether from the DSM. Opposition from several psychiatrists immediately followed. A referendum on the Board's decision was called, and in the spring of 1974, the entire membership of the APA was polled for their support or rejection of the Board's decision.[54]

4. Out of 10,000 voting members, nearly 40 percent opposed the Board's decision to normalize homosexuality.[55] Though the 40 percent were clearly a minority, and the decision was upheld, it showed how deeply divided the APA was on the matter.

5. The American Psychiatric Association, like the American Psychological Association, has since aligned itself heavily with gay causes,[56] furthering the impression that psychiatrists and psychologists in America generally view homosexuality as normal.

For these reasons, leaders within the gay Christian movement look to psychiatry for support when they claim that their orientation and behavior are normal.[57]

Response One: This argument is misleading in that it omits important facts surrounding the APA decision:

1. *The decision was not made under normal circumstances, but instead under remarkable duress in an intimidating environment.* In fact, it was made in the heat of grueling conflict, under threats of disruptions and intimidations, and the methods by which it was reached are questionable to this day. Recounting the events, Dr. Ronald Bayer, the author of the most comprehensive book on the subject, comments:

> The entire process, from the first confrontation organized by gay demonstrators to the referendum demanded by orthodox psychiatrists, seemed to violate the most basic expectations about how questions of science should be resolved. Instead of being engaged in sober discussion of data, psychiatrists were swept up in a political controversy. The result was not a conclusion based on an approximation of the scientific truth as dictated by reason, but was instead an action demanded by the ideological temper of the times.[58]

Considering Bayer's pro-gay sympathies, obviously displayed throughout his book, this admission on his part is remarkable.

2. *The APA did not state that homosexuality is normal.* The resolution that the APA Board of Trustees voted on in 1973 agreed that only clearly defined mental

disorders should be included in the DSM, and that if homosexuals felt no "subjective distress" about their sexuality and experienced no "impairment in social effectiveness or functioning," then their orientation should not be labeled as a disorder. The psychiatrist who authored the resolution, in fact, flatly denied that the APA was thereby saying homosexuality was normal.[59]

3. *The APA decision did not necessarily reflect the views of American psychiatrists.* A survey conducted by the journal *Medical Aspects of Homosexuality* in 1979 (six years after the APA decision) asked 10,000 psychiatrists if they felt homosexuality "usually represented a pathological adaptation." Sixty-nine percent of the respondents said "yes," and 60 percent said homosexual men were less capable of "mature, loving relationships" than heterosexual men.[60] Obviously, there remained a huge discrepancy between the American Psychiatric Association's official position and the views of many of its members.

Response Two: This argument is illogical in that it assumes that mental health and righteousness are one and the same.

Even if all members of the APA *had* agreed from the beginning that homosexuality was normal, and if all psychiatrists currently in practice viewed it as healthy, that has no bearing on the Christian position on the subject. The Bible speaks of homosexuality (as well as other sexual sins) in moral, not psychological, terms. In developing a sense of ethics, the Christian cannot take his cues from the mental health profession. What is deemed mentally sound by man may not be morally viable to God.

General Argument Four: Ten percent of the population is gay. Could so many people be wrong?

This argument has been so roundly disproven that it may be unnecessary to even mention it. But on the chance that the reader may need to confront it in future discussions, we will briefly review what is commonly called the "ten percent myth" and how to respond to it.

In 1948 sex researcher Alfred Kinsey published *Sexual Behavior in the Human Male*, which listed his findings after taking the sexual histories of 5,300 American men. The findings, especially on homosexuality, shocked American sensibilities: Thirty-seven percent of the subjects admitted at least one homosexual experience since their adolescence,[61] and ten percent claimed to have been homosexual for at least three years.[62]

The word was out—ten percent of the male population was homosexual! Knowing that there is power in numbers, pro-gay theorists and spokesmen repeated the statistic relentlessly until it became a given: One out of every ten males was gay; therefore, homosexuality was much commoner than anyone had previously thought. The concept was extremely useful to activists when, decades later, they'd ask how anyone could believe ten percent of the population was abnormal, immoral, or just plain wrong.

Response One: This argument is exaggerated. Kinsey did *not* claim ten percent of the male population was homosexual.

Kinsey's wording was plain—ten percent of the males surveyed claimed to have been homosexual for at least three years. They had not necessarily been homosexual all their lives, nor would they necessarily be homosexual in the future. Future studies by the Kinsey Institute, in fact, would confirm that sexual orientation is not necessarily fixed, and may change throughout a person's lifespan. *The 1990 Kinsey Institute New Report on Sex* states: "Some people have consistent homosexual orientation for a long period of time, then fall in love with a person of the opposite sex; other individuals who have had only opposite-sex partners later fall in love with someone of the same sex."[63]

Response Two: The "ten percent" figure is misleading for two reasons:

First, Kinsey's data was not taken from a population accurately representing American men. Dr. Judith Reisman, in her book *Kinsey, Sex and Fraud: The Indoctrination of a People*, has soundly discredited Kinsey's conclusions and methods. One of her important findings was that 25 percent of the men he surveyed were prisoners, many of whom were sex offenders.[64] Naturally, a higher incidence of homosexuality would be found among prisoners, especially sex offenders, many of whom may have been in prison for homosexual behavior. (In the 1940s that was quite possible; today, thankfully, people are not incarcerated for homosexuality.)

Second, subsequent studies have disproven the ten-percent claim. USA Today reported on April 15, 1993, a new survey of 3,321 American men indicating that 2.3 percent of them had engaged in homosexual behavior within the previous ten years; only 1.1 percent reported being exclusively homosexual.

This was only the latest in a series of studies proving Kinsey wrong. In 1989 a U.S. survey estimated that no more than six percent of adults had any same-sex contacts and only one percent were exclusively homosexual. A similar survey in France found that four percent of men and three percent of women had ever engaged in homosexual contacts, while only 1.4 percent of the men and 0.4 percent of the women had done so within the past five years. The article concluded, not surprisingly, that the ten percent statistic proposed by Kinsey was "dying under the weight of new studies."

A candid remark by a lesbian activist explains how the ten percent figure stayed in the public's awareness for so long:

> The thing about the "1 in 10"—I think people probably always did know that it was inflated. But it was a nice number that you could point to, that you could say "one in ten," and it's a

really good way to get people to visualize that we're here.[65]

If what she's saying is true, gay spokesmen were willing to repeat something they knew to be false, for the sake of furthering their cause. With that in mind, one wonders what other "facts" on homosexuality (for example, "gays are born gay," "gays cannot change") will someday be disproven as well, exposed as propaganda that people "always knew was inflated," but promoted anyway because the end justified the means.

We can accept some parts of these pro-gay arguments. We can allow, for example, the *possibility* of genetics someday being found to play a role in the development of homosexuality. We can agree that, in many cases, the homosexual condition—sexual attractions to the same sex rather than the opposite one—begins very early in life. And while it is common knowledge that ten percent of the population is not, nor ever has been, gay, we will admit that there are probably far more homosexuals in the population than we're aware of. Their claim of not having asked for their orientation is, in most cases, true; we ought to feel genuine compassion for people struggling with, or mistreated for, something they never chose. Stanton Jones of Wheaton College puts it well: "If you cannot empathize with a homosexual person because of fear of, or revulsion to, them, then you are failing our Lord."[66]

But where we must part company with promoters of the pro-gay theology is in the conclusions they have drawn. We cannot rewrite Scripture, as they have, to accommodate a sin simply because some believe it to be inborn, unchangeable, or common. On this point, we might well borrow a quote from, of all people, the liberal playwright Lillian Hellman: "I cannot and will not cut my conscience to suit this year's fashions."

Let's Talk About Social Justice and the Nature of Homosexuality

(A Sample Dialogue)

Gay Christian Argument: "How can you say it's wrong to be gay when it's been proven that gays are born that way! Do you think God made a mistake when He made me gay?"

Response: "Of course God didn't make a mistake when He made you, but why assume He made you gay?"

Gay Christian Argument: "Well, I sure didn't choose these feelings!"

Response: "Maybe not, but we *all* have feelings we don't choose. We all feel angry sometimes, or jealous, or we feel like lying, or having a sexual relationship with someone outside of marriage. Those feelings aren't a choice, but we *do* choose whether or not to *act* on them."

Gay Christian Argument: "But these aren't just minor temptations like the ones you just named. I've had them all my life. I was born with them, in fact!"

Response: "I beg to differ. I really don't believe homosexuality is inborn, but even if it is, that doesn't mean God intended it."

Gay Christian Argument: "You're saying my deepest feelings are wrong!?"

Response: "I'm saying we all have feelings—deep ones, at that—which aren't necessarily right, and which we shouldn't give in to."

Gay Christian Argument: "But I read a study that said my sexual feelings come from some variation in the hypothalamus. I can't do much about that, can I?"

Response: "I read that study, too, but no one's sure if it's accurate.

Gay Christian Argument: "Why do you say that?"

Response: "First, the study has never been replicated. And second, the researcher wasn't really sure which of his subjects were gay and which ones weren't, and he admits he doesn't know if the differences he found in brain sizes were the cause *of* homosexuality, or if they were caused *by* homosexuality. The scientific community isn't at all convinced he's proven anything."

Gay Christian Argument: "But there's another study on twins that seems to prove gays are born that way."

Response: "That one isn't too conclusive, either. Nearly half the identical twins studied didn't have the same sexual preference. Don't you think the percentage should have been higher? And none of those twins were raised apart, so who can tell what made them gay? Besides, none of the twin studies have been replicated, either. In fact, other twin studies have had completely different results."

Gay Christian Argument: "Well, I've felt gay all my life, so I must have been born this way!"

Response: "Maybe, or maybe it started so early you can't even remember it. Anyway, who says that "inborn" means "ideal"?

Gay Christian Argument: "So you think God might have given me these feelings and then expected me to resist them?"

Response: "Just because we've got feelings, doesn't mean God gave them to us. I've got feelings, too, that I have to resist. And I feel like I've had them all my life. It's not easy for me, either."

Gay Christian Argument: "Well, maybe you can do something about those feelings, but homosexuality can't be changed. All the psychologists agree on that."

Response: "Actually, they don't. Did you know there have always been, and still are, plenty of psychologists who think homosexuality can be changed, if the patient really wants that sort of change?"

Gay Christian Argument: "But I don't! Besides, even if I did, the only people who would do a thing like that would be right-wing fanatics."

Response: "There are plenty of credible therapists, non-Christian as well as Christian, who would help you if you wanted it."

Gay Christian Argument: "But I'm not sick, am I? Didn't the American Psychiatric Association say homosexuality is normal some 20 years ago?"

Response: "That's not exactly what they said. They *did* decide homosexuality wasn't a disorder, but they didn't quite say it was normal, either. Truthfully, politics played more into that decision than anyone realizes."

Gay Christian Argument: "Maybe so, but ten percent of the population couldn't possibly be mentally ill!"

Response: "I never said you're mentally ill. The Bible says homosexuality isn't *natural*; it doesn't say homosexuals are crazy. But if you're saying ten percent of the population is gay, I'm afraid that's way off. Every study done on the gay population, both here and abroad, shows it's much smaller than ten percent."

Gay Christian Argument: "Well, I don't believe God wants me to deny something I've had all my life—something I've tried to change, and something so many other people have, too. That just doesn't sound like God to me!"

Response: "That's funny. It sounds *exactly* like God to me. And it sounds like He requires of you the same things He requires of all of us. He asks us to deny something we've had all our lives—our *selves*—and take up our crosses daily to follow Him. He knows we've tried to change ourselves, and He knows we can't! But Jesus never said we had to change ourselves. He told us to follow Him, and to live obediently. The inward change is up to Him, but the obedience is up to us. Plenty of other people have 'selves' too, by the way. They may choose to indulge their selves, but as Christians, we're called to something different. We're not here to satisfy our selves. We're here to lose them! In the long run, that's the only way to really find ourselves, anyway."

8

Society's Response
to Homosexuality

*"Gay is proud and gay is loud and gay is get-
ting louder—What are you going to say in the
dialogue that we are ready to enter into?"*
— Gay activist addressing a
panel of psychiatrists

I faced a dilemma as a gay Christian: most of
society believed I was wrong. That could not
be ignored. Every day I saw or heard something that reminded me that homosexuality was abnormal, immoral, unequal to heterosexuality. (Eighteen
years later that hasn't changed. Americans still, by and
large, disapprove of homosexuality.[1])

Having struggled so hard to accept my identity, I was
not about to reject it again. But the tension between society and me had to be resolved. One of us had to be wrong,
and I had already decided it wasn't me. So I needed to
convince myself that society erred in its beliefs about, and
treatment of, homosexuals.

It wasn't too hard finding evidence to support my belief. Prejudice against gays would crop up occasionally—

133

a "fag" joke overheard in the lunchroom at work, graffiti scrawled on the walls of my favorite gay bar, newspaper accounts of yet another gay man assaulted. All I needed to do was convince myself that prejudice was more than occasional—that it was *everywhere*, lurking behind every negative view of homosexuality, no matter how reasonably that view was expressed. Thus *all* objections to homosexuality were, in my mind, born of bigotry or misunderstanding. That made those objections easy to write off as "prejudice," and my comfort with myself would stay intact.

I don't believe I'm the only one who has done that. Listening to gay Christian arguments today, I can still hear the need to make society wrong, and to prohibit any views that challenge the pro-gay position. This can be done in three basic ways:

1. By insisting homophobia is the *only* reason people object to homosexuality.

2. By discrediting preachers who speak against homosexuality, accusing them of inciting violence against gays and lesbians.

3. By claiming that young homosexuals may take their own lives if they hear people saying that their orientation is unnatural. (This is a sure way to inhibit honest dialogue on the subject.)

Each of these arguments will be used against anyone who confronts the gay Christian movement. For this reason, each of them will be explored in detail.

General Argument One: Homophobia is the problem, not homosexuality.

Some words have a chilling effect—"sexist" or "racist," for example. In their original use, they described attitudes we should abhor. Today, though, their meaning changes to suit the agenda of whoever is using them. A man defending abortion may label pro-lifers as "sexist" for wanting to deny a woman's "right to choose."

A woman opposed to affirmative action programs may find herself accused of being "racist." Negative labels stick. The person they're stuck to loses credibility, even when he or she has something important to say. Who, after all, values a bigot's opinion?

In this manner, *homophobia* has been used to tarnish any objection to homosexuality. The word itself is relatively new, coined in 1972 by psychologist George Weinberg, referring to the "dread of being in close quarters with homosexuals."[2] Its meaning has expanded to include, according to Dr. Joseph Nicolosi, "any belief system that values heterosexuality as superior to and/or more natural than homosexuality."[3] By that standard, no conservative Christian escapes the homophobia label; neither do most other people, religious and nonreligious alike.

Still, when the term is used in discussions today, it is seldom defined. People throw it at their opponents, judging them guilty of homophobia, without telling them exactly what homophobia is and exactly how they are guilty of being whatever it is. So instead of simply denying I am homophobic (which usually gets me nowhere), I've found it helpful to discuss the word itself, making an intelligent discussion of it more likely. So once the term "homophobia" is thrown out as the "problem," it's best to begin with a response to the term itself.

Response One: The argument ("homophobia is the problem, not homosexuality") is misleading for two reasons:

1. *The argument implies a phobic condition that the accused most likely does not really have.* A phobia, according to the American Psychiatric Association, is defined as "an irrational dread or fear of object or activity, leading to significant avoidance of the dreaded object" (*Diagnostic and Statistical Manual*).

In the recent comedy film *What About Bob?* a psychiatric patient is beset with phobias, claustrophobia being one of them. When approaching a small space, such as an elevator or crowded bus, he psyches himself up, mutters under his breath, and tries (usually unsuccessfully) to endure being in a small space even for a short time.

Assuming that homosexuality is the "object or activity" the homophobe dreads, shouldn't all us "homophobes" be like Bob? When seeing a homosexual, if we are truly homophobic, shouldn't we, too, have to psyche ourselves up, muttering under our breath, barely enduring the presence of a homosexual even for a short time?

Yet we don't. So it is unlikely that the person being accused of homophobia is truly homophobic. To be so, according to the APA, the person would have to dread homosexuality or homosexuals, taking pains to avoid both.

The Christian woman or man who speaks face to face with homosexuals—whether in confrontations or discussions—or works alongside them, or relates to them in any way, could hardly be said to have a "phobic response" to them. In the strictest sense, then, few people can truly be called "homophobic." Their feelings toward homosexuals may be negative, but that, in itself, does not constitute a phobia.

2. *The argument prematurely assumes that negative reactions to homosexuality are phobias.* I have come to believe that most negative reactions to homosexuality stem not from homophobia, but from one of two sources: prejudice or convictions.

Webster defines prejudice as an "opinion against something without adequate basis." By that definition, there's a great deal of prejudice against homosexuals. They are automatically disliked—despised, even—by people who have formed opinions about them with no rational basis. Prejudice hurts; it's unfair and mean-spirited in the extreme. But it's not a phobia, as in a "dread" or "fear." It is a sin, and a vile one, at that.

By contrast, "conviction," according to Webster, "is a state of being convinced; a strong belief." It is entirely possible to have a strong belief about homosexuality without prejudice or phobia. That, I believe, is the case with most Christians. Even Mel White, who throughout his book condemns homophobia in the church, agrees that "thoughtful students of the Scriptures may disagree on the subject of homosexuality."[4]

Andrew Sullivan, the gay editor of *The New Republic*, goes even further by saying:

> Perhaps the most depressing and fruitless fea-
> ture of the current debate about homosexual-
> ity is to treat all versions of this [conservative
> Christian] argument as the equivalent of big-
> otry. They are not. At its most serious, it [the
> Christian prohibition against homosexuality]
> is not a phobia; it is an argument.[5]

My admiration for one of my favorite actors has helped me understand the difference between a phobia, prejudice, and conviction. There is no one I enjoy watching more on the screen than Spencer Tracy. In all his films, he exuded a combination of integrity, cynicism, dry wit, and kindness. He was a rare breed—a true gentleman with a "don't even think of messing with me" attitude. I loved his films; I respect his work.

I also know he was an adulterer. For years he carried on an affair with Katherine Hepburn, even though he was married. And, knowing adultery is biblically condemned, I make no bones about the immorality of Tracy and Hepburn's relationship.

Does that make me "Tracy-phobic?" Hardly! I couldn't enjoy watching someone I had a phobic response to, any more than an arachnophobic could enjoy watching a spider.

Perhaps, then, it makes me guilty of prejudice, having an opinion about Tracy without adequate basis? Again, no. There is a specific basis for my belief about adultery, but that in no way interferes with my respect for the man in other areas. I have a conviction about adultery: *it's wrong*. Tracy committed it, so, in that area, I say he was wrong. I also say he was terrific in other ways.

The same can be said about Elton John, K. D. Lange, Martina Navratilova, Greg Louganis, and Johnny Mathis, all of whom are openly homosexual. Their contributions have enriched us; their achievements are remarkable. Not only is it *possible* to appreciate them while disagreeing with them; it's downright illogical *not* to.

In short, the term homophobia can be used accurately in very few cases. "Prejudice" describes unfounded negative attitudes toward homosexuals, while "conviction" describes the beliefs of people holding the conservative Christian view of homosexuality.

General Argument Two: Preaching against homosexuality incites violence against lesbians and gay men.

In Roger Biery's *Understanding Homosexuality: The Pride and the Prejudice*, a devastated parent describes the death of his gay son during an altercation with a policeman:

> The cop said that he flashed a badge and that my son flashed a knife, a switchblade. They fought and my son was killed. If all this was true, why was our son carved up like a turkey? Our son never had a knife. He never hurt anyone. That Anita Bryant witch and her mob helped kill him. She spread enough hate to kill lots of kids. Gave the crazies an excuse to witch hunt.[6]

Exactly who was at fault cannot be proven. It is not for us to explore the allegations this man makes against the police. But his allegations against Anita Bryant— and, by extension, all of us taking a public stand against the gay rights movement—need to be taken seriously.

Does teaching that homosexuality is wrong, or preaching against homosexual behavior, or speaking publicly
against pro-gay laws, as Anita Bryant did, really "help
kill," "spread hate," and give "crazies" an excuse to go on
a witch-hunt? I'm convinced it does not. But this argument deserves careful consideration. If we care at all
about homosexuals, we cannot be indifferent to charges
that we are in any way harming them.

**Response One: This argument is misleading and il-
logical because it assumes that religious teaching is
responsible for violent behavior. There are three reasons to believe it is not:**
First, there is a world of difference between *belief*
and *bigotry*. Teaching and preaching moral *beliefs* does
not incite violence. If it did, every time a pastor preached
on the evils of lying, cheating, or fornicating, his parishioners would leave the sanctuary and attack the first
liar, tax evader, or fornicator they ran into. Logic tells
us, then, that preaching or speaking against a certain
sin cannot, in itself, move people to attack the person
committing the sin.
Second, violent bigotry needs no teaching or preaching in order to survive. Racists on the prowl for minorities to attack don't need a sermon to get them going;
their hatred is motivation enough. Likewise, "gay bashers" (people who commit acts of violence against homosexuals) need no sermon on the evils of homosexuality
to motivate their actions. Seldom if ever have gay bashers approached a victim saying, "We just came from
church and heard you're a sinner, so we're going to assault you."
Third, religious beliefs *can* be used as a cover for bigotry, and as an excuse for violence. White supremacists
mangle the Bible to justify their hate. Nazis referred to
Jewish people as "Christ-killers," giving them yet another
excuse for their anti-Semitism. This is also true of people
who assault homosexuals—they may use religious beliefs

as a cover for their hatred, but it is their *hatred*, not their beliefs, that incites their violence.

Mel White provides a good example of this, perhaps unintentionally, in *Stranger at the Gate*. Criticizing the Christian community as "the nation's primary source of antigay bigotry and discrimination," he then relates the story of an author who, in writing about the murder of a homosexual, interviewed young men who had been found guilty of hate crimes against gays and lesbians.

"In far too many cases," he says, "those young men came from Christian homes and families."[7] Citing another study on violence against gays, he continues: "Available studies show that those who attend church more regularly and are more 'orthodox,' 'devout,' or 'fundamentalist' tend to be more disapproving [of gay and lesbian people]."[8]

Though it seems that White is attempting to show how religious disapproval of homosexuality leads to violence against homosexuals, he makes, in fact, a good case for the opposite position. The studies he mentions seem to prove that such teaching does *not*, by itself, incite violence.

If it did, these young "gay bashers" from Christian homes would not have been convicted of hate crimes against homosexuals alone; they'd have also been found guilty of hate crimes against adulterers, gossips, drunks, idolators, rebellious teenagers, and believers who didn't carefully examine their hearts before taking Holy Communion. Why? Because *all* of these things are also preached against in church and in Christian homes.

Furthermore, if fundamentalist, devout, orthodox Christian teaching on homosexuality inspires violence against homosexuals, shouldn't the majority of children raised in Christian homes be out assaulting homosexuals? To be sure, even one person attacking one homosexual is one too many. But why are the youths cited in White's book the exception rather than the rule? If Christian teaching against homosexuality inspires hatred and violence toward homosexuals, then the majority of people raised in Christian homes should both hate and assault gays.

But they don't. Those raised in Christian homes who do attack homosexuals are seriously disturbed. Their beliefs are incidental; they may use them as an excuse, but their illness, not their religion, fuels their behavior. There is no reason to believe they would behave any differently if they'd never heard religious teaching on homosexuality, just as there is no reason to assume Nazis would hate Jewish people any less if they didn't have the "Christ-killer" teaching to hang their hatred on. John Boswell provides a relevant quote on doctrine being used as a mask for preexisting hate: "We can easily reduce our detractors to absurdity and show them their hostility is groundless. But what does this prove? That their hatred is *real*. Intolerance itself will remain finally irrefutable."[9]

General Argument Three: Preaching against homosexuality causes gay adolescent suicides

> No one knew why. Her boyfriend found the answer when the high school principal let him clean out her locker. Scribbled notes in the rear flap of her binder told her story. She was gay and she knew it, but her mother had been active in crusading against gay rights. She knew nothing positive about gay people, believed she had been cursed, and dared not disgrace the family. And so she killed herself. That mother mourns her daughter in mystery still, not knowing that she helped to kill her.[10]

The plight of gay teenagers, and the specter of gay adolescent suicide, haunts anyone familiar with the subject. No one, regardless of their beliefs about homosexuality, wants to see young lives destroyed. So, in light of stories like this one, and the author's contention that a mother's opposition to gay rights killed her daughter, we are forced to ask ourselves: Does standing or preaching against homosexuality damage adolescents who may be struggling with their own sexuality?

Gay counseling programs in the public school system certainly seem to think so. High school English teacher John Anderson, stressing the need for school-sponsored gay support, writes: "How people interpret the Bible is another part of the problem. Some pick and choose their way through the Bible and select passages that condemn homosexual activity."[11]

Counseling workshops in the public schools agree. When discussing how to create an "affirmative environment" for gay students, a group of Arizona public school counselors and nurses had a clear goal:

> Homophobia must be eliminated. Homophobia was touted by a clear majority of those in attendance as stemming mostly from the religious Christian community whose ignorance and "misrepresentation of the Bible to justify their prejudice" was the cause of hatred towards, crimes against, and even the deaths of young homosexuals.[12]

Hearing this, the average Christian may well be tempted to never say a word against homosexuality again! It's horrible to think that our words could cause someone's death. We would rather stay mute than see a child kill himself because of something we said. And, of course, that fear can be exploited by its promoters, intimidating us from taking any kind of stand on the issue.

Once, during a conference on homosexuality and the church, a visibly enraged young man shouted at me (and all the other guest speakers) that we should watch our words more carefully. "When you say homosexuality's wrong, young people hear what you say and wind up killing themselves!"

I tried to politely inform him that we cared about young people as much as he did, and that simple logic tells us that saying a thing is *wrong* is a far cry from saying that the people who do that thing should *kill themselves*. But he would have none of it; he'd already decided that teaching against homosexual behavior inspired teen suicides; therefore, the blood of gay teenagers was on our hands.

I have heard variations of his argument several times: "When you say homosexuality is wrong, you teach young gays to hate themselves, you lower their self-esteem, you push them toward suicide." (One publication I read went so far as to say that it is child abuse to teach your children that heterosexuality is normal!)

Whether or not they mean to, the people who use these arguments are using the crudest form of manipulation. Like the homophobia argument, or the argument that preaching against homosexuality incites violence, this argument stifles free speech in the name of "concern for our children." But saying that our view of homosexuality damages gay teens is a pretty strong accusation. It needs to be examined before it is accepted.

The belief that gay teenagers are at high risk of suicide, and that telling them homosexuality is abnormal increases that risk, is largely inspired by a 1989 report by a special federal task force on youth and suicide. Presented to Dr. Louis Sullivan, former Secretary of Health and Human Services, the report concluded that:

1. Gay and lesbian youths account for one-third of all teenage suicides.

2. Suicide is the leading cause of death among gay teenagers.

3. Gay teenagers who commit suicide do so because of "internalized homophobia" and violence directed at them.

Later in the report, traditional fundamentalist and Catholic homes are admonished to recognize how they "contribute to the rejection of gay youth by their families and suicide among gay male youth."[13] This report, and its conclusions, has been repeated over and over again, in gay and mainstream publications. For this reason, many gays and gay Christian advocates (and many in the general population, as well) believe that traditional teaching on homosexuality contributes to the death of homosexual teenagers.

Response: This argument is misleading for three basic reasons:

1. *The report's statistical data and numerical conclusions are highly questionable.* The report this argument is based on was conducted by a San Francisco gay activist named Paul Gibson, whose research was so shoddy that Dr. Sullivan, to whom it was submitted, officially distanced himself and his department from it, stating that it did not in any way represent his personal beliefs or the policy of his department. For Dr. Sullivan to so repudiate a study submitted to his department means he must have found some serious flaws in it.

And indeed he did. Peter LaBarbera, a former reporter for the *Washington Times* and editor of the *Lambda Report*, researched Gibson's report and found numerous flaws. In what follows I'll paraphrase the evidence LaBarbera came up with.

First, to bolster his claim about the prevalence of gay suicides, Gibson quotes an author who speculated in 1985 that "as many as 3,000 gay youths kill themselves each year." That figure exceeds the total number of annual teen suicides by more than 1,000![14]

As if that exaggeration were not bad enough, Gibson then padded his figure when he asserted that gay teenagers account for one-third of all adolescent suicides. He studied assorted gay surveys on troubled and runaway youth, found the rate of suicidal tendencies (not even actual suicides) among the gay teenagers in the surveys, then multiplied the figure by ten percent, using the discredited Kinsey figure to determine how many gay teenagers commit suicide! This led David Shaffer, a Columbia University psychiatrist and specialist on adolescent suicide, to remark: "I struggled for a long time over Gibson's mathematics, but, in the end, it seemed more hocus-pocus than math."[15]

And yet it is on the basis of this faulty data that gay teenage counseling programs are developed across the country, and gay teenagers are assumed to be at high risk of suicide, and Christian parents are accused of damaging gay children!

2. *The report's conclusions about gay teenage suicides are contradicted by other, more credible reports.* A 1986 study of San Diego youth conducted by the University of California, San Diego, interviewed the survivors of 238 suicide attempts, 133 of which were under 30. Only nine (or seven percent) were found to have been homosexual, none of whom were under 21. These results are light-years away from Gibson's.

Additionally, in a Columbia University study of 107 New York male teen suicides, only three were known to have been homosexual, and two of those died in a suicide pact. Other research conducted by the Gallup organization on 1,152 teenagers found that, out of the 60 percent who knew a teen who had committed suicide, not one mentioned the teen's sexuality as being a part of the problem. And of those who had come close to killing themselves, most cited boy/girl problems or low self-esteem (not homosexuality) as the cause.[16]

3. *No heterosexual control group was used in Gibson's study.* Amazingly, Gibson had the audacity to submit his conclusions about gay teen suicide to Dr. Sullivan (and to the public) without having used a heterosexual control group for comparison. How, then, could he possibly have known to what extent homosexuality played a factor in these suicides without a comparison group? David Shaffer, whose experience with teenage suicide cases is vast, found little difference between the case histories of Gibson's gay teen suicides and the majority of other teen suicides he's studied: "The stories were the same: a court appearance scheduled for the day of the death; prolonged depression; drug and alcohol problems; etc."[17]

In other words, the problems the gay suicidal teenagers faced were similar to those of other distressed teens. If prejudice against homosexuals factored into their tragic deaths, it certainly does not show up in the evidence.

Nevertheless, gay counseling programs across the nation are cropping up, largely in response to this discredited report that states, but cannot prove, the prevalence of gay teenage suicides. If nothing else, Gibson has achieved a real coup: he concocted a problem, reported on it, then came up with an action plan to solve it.

Of course, some gay teens commit suicide. Heterosexual teens do as well. Anything we can do to prevent these tragedies must be done. But it is blatantly self-serving, if not downright cruel, for gays or their sympathizers to suggest that Christian teaching is somehow responsible for the isolation, mistreatment, and death of a child. As in the case of violence aimed against gays in general, the blame for this must be placed elsewhere.

But that does not leave us blameless. Standing for biblical values has by no means contributed to the death or emotional damage of homosexuals. But the way we have stood for those values may be another matter. Regardless of how often we claim to hate the sin but love the sinner, many of us need to ask ourselves just how that "love for the sinner" has been expressed.

In 1981 Professor Richard Lovelace at Gordon-Conwell Theological Seminary commented, in *Christianity Today* magazine, "Most of the repenting that needs to be done on the issue of homosexuality needs to be done by straight people, including straight Christians. By far the greater sin in our church is the sin of neglect, fear, hatred."[18]

Many Christians, of course, and many churches, have opened their doors and hearts to homosexuals. They have loved them, without compromising the Bible's standards, and by speaking the truth in love, they've seen gays and lesbians won into the kingdom of God.

But not all pastors and congregations can say the same, which brings us to a crucial point: If homosexuals have found rejection and isolation in society, then come into our sanctuaries, only to find no sanctuary at all but more rejection, then the judgment we so eagerly pronounce on them for their perversion of sex will no doubt fall on us as well—perhaps a hundredfold—for our perversion of the gospel.

Let's Talk About Society's Response to Homosexuality

(A Sample Dialogue)

Gay Christian Advocate: "When you say homosexuality is wrong, you're really expressing the same old problem: *homophobia.*"
Response: "What exactly is homophobia?"

Gay Christian Argument: "Homophobia is the unreasonable fear or hatred of gays, and it's everywhere. Our whole society is saturated with it."
Response: "That sounds horrible. And if people have hated or feared you, I'm sorry to hear it. No one should be treated that way. But tell me, exactly how have I done that to you?"

Gay Christian Argument: "By using the Bible verses to condemn me whenever you talk about homosexuality!"
Response: "But I believe the Bible. You say, as a gay Christian, that you believe it, too. Doesn't that mean we both take our moral guidance from Scripture?"

Gay Christian Argument: "Yes."
Response: "Then what's wrong with quoting it when I explain why I believe homosexuality is wrong?"

Gay Christian Argument: "Because most people who quote the Bible to gays are homophobic, and they're using the Bible as an excuse to hate us."
Response: "That's a strong accusation. Am I acting like I hate you? I believe homosexuality's wrong, sure. But

that's a belief, not a phobia. If I was homophobic, could I be sitting here talking to you? After all, if I had a phobia about gays, I'd be afraid to be anywhere near you!"

Gay Christian Argument: "But you think homosexuality's a big sin or something."

Response: "I think it's a sin, no worse or better than some of my own sins. But thinking something is a sin, and having a phobia about it, are two very different things."

Gay Christian Argument: "But don't you know how many lesbians and gays get beaten up because people like you go around saying it's a sin?"

Response: "I'm against anyone getting hurt, and I'll speak out against gay bashing as much as I'll speak out against gay practices. But nobody gets beat up just because I, or any other Christian, says homosexuality is a sin."

Gay Christian Argument: "Oh, yes they do! Studies show that gay bashers come from religious homes, just like yours."

Response: "Some do, but it's their own craziness, not religion that makes them do those terrible things. Some murderers and rapists also come from Christian homes, but that doesn't mean their religious upbringing made them commit their crimes. Thinking homosexuality is wrong doesn't make you beat homosexuals up. I think it's wrong, and I'm not beating you up, am I?"

Gay Christian Argument: "No, but if I was a teenager, the things you say about gays would really hurt me. Gay teenagers hear people like you speak and they learn to hate themselves. Lots of them even commit suicide!"

Response: "If gay teenagers learn to hate themselves, it's not because they hear people like me speak.

I don't call gays names, or make fun of them, or say they're worse than anybody else."

Gay Christian Argument: "But when you say homosexuality is sinful, they just soak that in and think there's something wrong with themselves!"

Response: "Are you saying that every time we teach morality, teenagers are damaged? That doesn't make sense. Teaching something is wrong doesn't make kids feel terrible about themselves. If it did, we'd be damaging them every time we taught them not to steal, or lie, or cheat. And as for homosexual teenagers committing suicide, well, that's a horrible thing if it happens even once. But the problem is being exaggerated. I'm not saying it doesn't happen; just that it doesn't happen nearly as much as some people say it does."

Gay Christian Argument: "But it does happen!"

Response: "Yes, and we should work together to prevent it. But silencing the Christian view of homosexuality isn't the way to do it. Parents have the right to teach values to their children without the school interfering. Besides, there's no solid evidence that religious teaching causes kids to harm themselves."

Gay Christian Argument: "Yes, there is! A study came out a few years ago proving that gay kids are three times more likely to kill themselves than straight kids are. And when they do, they often do it because of people like you with your antigay viewpoint."

Response: "The study you're talking about has been completely discredited. The Secretary of Health and Human Services wouldn't touch it, it was so bad. None of the claims it made have been proven, and several of them have been disproven."

Gay Christian Argument: "Such as?"

Response: "Such as the idea that gay teens are three times more likely to kill themselves. Repeated studies have shown that's false. And not once has it been proven that religious teaching on homosexuality increases the likelihood of a teenager committing suicide. So, you see, it's a serious thing you're accusing me of. You're laying the deaths of gay teenagers at my feet, saying I'm somehow responsible. That's not fair, and it's certainly inaccurate.

The fact is, you and I have a completely different view of homosexuality. I can live with that. But I would ask, with all due respect, that you not accuse me of things I've never done—things like hurting teenagers, or spreading prejudice. Because when you do that, you're guilty of the very thing you say conservative Christians do to you. You're spreading myths and stereotypes. We may not agree on homosexuality, but I'm sure we both agree on the need to be truthful, even when we disagree."

9

General Religious Arguments

"What is being depicted to individuals is a 'user-friendly' God who will smile benignly down upon their lifestyles of choice,as they continue to live as they like."

— Greg Laurie, "The Great Compromise "

We'd rather be nice.

There is a strange tendency creeping into the church: "Niceness" is taking precedence over truth. Immorality—even among Christian leaders—is going unconfronted; doctrinal lines are fuzzier than ever; and many churches seem more concerned with making people comfortable than arousing in them a sense of their need for God.

All of this needs to be acknowledged before we confront the gay Christian movement. Much of the criticism we level at them needs to be sent our way, as well.

For example, while reading Mel White's *Stranger at the Gate*, I was struck by his description of the Metropolitan Community Church he had begun attending: "When I asked Ken (the gay pastor) why he never preached about sin or judgment, but only about God's love and grace, he smiled and answered without hesitation, 'The people who come to this church have heard enough about sin and judgment.'"[1]

How typical of a gay church, I thought. *No preaching on sin—just grace without responsibility.*

Not three days later, though, I ran across information proving that this pastor's unbalanced approach wasn't unique to gay churches. Reluctance to discuss sin—much less confront it—is widespread among Christians. Truth is taking a back seat to accommodation.

A recent poll showed that 66 percent (two-thirds) of Americans no longer believe there is such a thing as "absolute truth." More distressing, though, was the fact that 53 percent of those not believing in absolute truth identified themselves as being born-again Christians—75 percent of whom were mainline Protestants.[2]

If absolute truth no longer exists, even in the minds of half the born-again population, it logically follows that doctrine, and the Bible itself, is given less credence. Pollster George Gallup, Jr. noticed this in *The People's Religion: American Faith in the 90s.* "While religion is highly popular in America," he states, "it is to a large extent superficial. There is a knowledge gap between America's stated faith and the lack of the most basic knowledge about that faith."[3]

In short, self-identified Christians in the 90s are biblically ignorant. Doctrine has become less important than good feelings; indeed, a *USA Today* survey found that, of the 56 percent of Americans who attend church, 45 percent did so because "it's good for you," 26 percent went for peace of mind. Specific doctrines, the pollster noted, seemed unimportant.[4]

If the notions of "truth" and "doctrine" are becoming unimportant to Christians, can the idea of "sin" hope to survive? Probably not. Twenty-five percent of Christians polled in 1993 believed sin to be "an outdated concept."[5]

"The awareness of sin used to be our shadow," Cornelius Plantinga writes in *Christianity Today.* "Christians hated sin, feared it, flew from it. But now the shadow has faded. Nowadays, the accusation *you have sinned* is often said with a grin."[6]

But the gospel truth is never so accommodating. John the Baptist was ferocious with the Pharisees (Matthew 3:7-8); Jesus trounced Peter when he tried to interfere with His mission (Matthew 16:22-23); and Paul was willing to publicly rebuke hypocrisy, even when committed by a respected disciple (Galatians 2:11-14). To be sure, there is a place for gentleness. But never at the expense of truth.

Yet today the gap between truth and modern practice has been large enough to allow any number of false (albeit "nice") ideas to enter the church, creating a mentality that says *Let's all get along without conflict, shall we?* Author J. Stephen Lang attempts to explain this phenomenon: "Love is understandable—warm and fuzzy. Doctrine, on the other hand, sounds cold, difficult, and demanding."[7]

A desire for "warm and fuzzy" without a commitment to truth makes the general religious arguments of the pro-gay theology all the more palatable. Unlike the social justice arguments of the previous chapters, these arguments are more "religious"—that is, they appeal to general religious themes of harmony and goodwill, while bypassing issues of the fallen nature, sin, and obedience. To the biblically ignorant they can pass for truth; in the light of Scripture, though, they have no leg to stand on.

Since they are more religious in tone than social arguments, they can be answered almost exclusively in biblical terms. Remembering that members of the gay Christian movement say they believe in biblical authority, these arguments are best answered with a call to return to the objective truth of the Bible, in lieu of the subjective winds of human experience and understanding.

General Religious Argument One: Jesus said nothing about homosexuality.

This one is a favorite at gay parades. Invariably, when the gay Christian movement is represented, someone in their group will hold up a sign saying:

```
WHAT JESUS SAID
ABOUT HOMOSEXUALITY:
```

The idea, of course, is that if Jesus did not specifically forbid a behavior, then the behavior must not have been important to Him. Stretching the point further, this argument assumes that if Jesus was not manifestly concerned about something, we shouldn't be, either.

Troy Perry is typical of gay Christian leaders in making much of this argument based on silence: "As for the question 'What did Jesus say about homosexuality?' the answer is simple. Jesus said nothing. Not one thing. Nothing! Jesus was more interested in love."[8] So, according to the argument of silence, if Jesus didn't talk about it, neither should we.

Response: This argument is misleading and illogical for four reasons:

First, the argument assumes that the Gospels are more authoritative than the rest of the books in the Bible. The idea of a subject being unimportant just because it was not mentioned by Jesus is foreign to the Gospel writers themselves. At no point did Matthew, Mark, Luke, or John say their books should be elevated above the Torah or, for that matter, any writings yet to come. In other words, the Gospels—and the teachings they contain—are not more important than the rest of the

Bible. *All* Scripture is given by inspiration of God (2 Timothy 3:16). The same Spirit that inspired the authors of the Gospels also inspired the men who wrote the rest of the Bible.

Second, the argument assumes that the Gospels are more comprehensive than they really are. Not only are the Gospels no more authoritative than the rest of Scripture, they're not comprehensive either. That is, they do not provide all we need to know by way of doctrine and practical instruction.

Some of the Bible's most important teachings, in fact, does not appear in the gospels. The doctrine of man's old and new nature, outlined by Paul in Romans 6; the future of Israel and the mystery of the Gentiles, hinted at by Christ but explained more fully in Romans 9 through 11; the explanation and management of the spiritual gifts detailed in 1 Corinthians 12 and 14; the priesthood of Christ illustrated in Hebrews—*all of these appear after the Gospel accounts of Christ's life, death, and resurrection.* (And we're not even mentioning the entire Old Testament!) Would anyone say these doctrines are unimportant simply because they weren't mentioned by Jesus?

Or, put another way, are we really to believe that Jesus didn't care about wife-beating or incest, just because He said nothing about them? Aren't the prohibitions against incest in Leviticus and 1 Corinthians, as well as Paul's admonition to husbands to love their wives, enough to instruct us in these matters without being mentioned in the Gospels? There are any number of evil behaviors Jesus did not mention by name; surely we don't condone them for that reason alone!

Likewise, Christ's silence on homosexuality in no way negates the very specific prohibitions against it which appear elsewhere, in both the Old and New Testaments.

Third, this argument is inaccurate in that it presumes to know all of what Jesus said. The Gospels do not profess to be complete accounts of Jesus' life and teachings.

Whole sections of His early years are omitted; much of what He did and said remains unknown.

Luke wrote his gospel so Theophilus would "know the certainty of those things, wherein thou hast been instructed" (Luke 1:4). John's motives are broader: "These are written, that ye might believe that Jesus is the Christ, the Son of God; and that believing ye might have life through his name" (John 20:31). But none of these authors suggested they were recording *all* of Christ's words.

John, in fact, said that would have been an impossibility: "And there are also many other things which Jesus did, which, if they should be written every one, I suppose that even the world itself could not contain the books that should be written" (John 21:25).

If that's the case, how can we be certain He said nothing about homosexuality? No one can say. But we know there are other equally important subjects left undiscussed in the Gospels, but mentioned in detail in other books of the Bible. Homosexuality, while absent from Matthew, Mark, Luke, and John, is conspicuously present in both Testaments and, just as conspicuously, it is forbidden.

Fourth, this argument wrongly assumes that because Jesus said nothing specifically about homosexuality, He said nothing about heterosexuality as a standard. In Mark 10:5-9, Jesus spoke in the most specific terms about God's created intent for human sexuality: "From the beginning of the creation God made them male and female. For this cause shall a man leave his father and mother, and cleave to his wife; and they twain shall be one flesh . . . What therefore God hath joined together, let not man put asunder."

In this passage, Jesus had been presented with a hypothetical question: Was divorce lawful? Instead of giving a simple "yes" or "no," He referred to the Genesis account and, more specifically, to *created intent* as the standard by which to judge sexual matters. By citing Genesis, He emphasized several key elements of the created intent for marriage and sexual relating: Independence was one—a man was to leave his own home to establish his own family with his wife; a "one flesh" sexual union (between *male and female, man and wife*) was another; and, of course, monogamy.

Homosexuality may not have been mentioned by Jesus; many other sexual variations weren't, either. But He couldn't have spelled out the standard for sexual expression more clearly: *male to female*, joined as God intended them to be. He can't be assumed to have approved of anything less.

General Religious Argument Two: "I'm a born-again believer *and* I'm gay. How can that be, if homosexuality is wrong?"

This argument is most often promoted by a declaration: *I'm gay and Christian, which is living proof that you can be both!* Mel White, upon his installation as dean of America's largest gay congregation, made a similar affirmation: "Now, thank God, after 30 years of struggle, I can say at last who I really am. I am gay. I am proud. And God loves me without reservation."[9] The message, then, is that if a person is truly born again and homosexual, the two must be compatible.

Response: This argument is illogical in that it assumes that if one is a Christian, and if one is loved by God, then what one does must be all right in God's sight.

We can assume that Dr. White's assertions are true: He is gay, he says he is proud (and no one is in a position to say otherwise), and God loves him. But does God's love for him, or White's pride in being gay, justify homosexuality itself?

Hardly. And while it is beyond the scope of this book to enter into the debate over eternal security ("once saved, always saved"), let's remember that Christians do not automatically become non-Christians just because they're sinning. The fact that they are sinning—even if they don't realize it—does not automatically nullify their salvation.

But neither does their salvation legitimize their sin. A Christian may, indeed, be openly homosexual. But that's no proof that homosexuality and Christianity are compatible. In fact, a Christian may be openly sinning; that's no proof that sin and Christianity are compatible either.

Ananias and Sapphira, a husband and wife mentioned in Acts 5, were evidently believers. Yet their sin of hypocrisy (pretending to give more money to the church than they actually did) cost them their lives. They were Christians, and they were in serious error. Their error did not mean they weren't Christian; their Christianity did not legitimize their error.

Peter was, on at least one occasion, afraid to be seen associating with Gentiles, for fear of reprisals from Jews who felt that Jews and Gentiles should never mix. So when Jewish people were not around, he was willing to eat with Gentile friends; when Jews were present, he avoided Gentiles (Galatians 2:11-13). His hypocrisy in the face of prejudice was wrong, yet no one doubts he was a Christian. That in no way justified his hypocrisy.

In other words, being a Christian is no indication, in itself, that your life is pleasing to God. Any honest believer knows that.

Most of the people I knew, while working at the Metropolitan Community Church, were from conservative backgrounds like mine. They had come from Baptist, Pentecostal, or fundamentalist churches where they'd had a genuine conversion experience. Yet we all had decided that homosexuality was acceptable and, to the best of my knowledge, we did not become non-Christians the moment we made that decision. (I will leave it to others to determine at what point we might have lost our salvation, if that is possible.) For all intents and purposes, we were Christians, and we were homosexual.

We were also wrong. Deceived, rebellious, or ignorant—the fact remains that we were wrong. That's where the discussion should focus—on ethics, not experience. Instead of arguing whether or not a Christian can be homosexual, or vice versa, the primary question should be whether homosexuality itself is right or wrong.

It is a waste of time to argue intangibles, such as whether or not a "gay Christian" is *truly* born again, or "saved." We may argue that if he continues in sin, he risks hardening his heart toward God, or reaping corruption, since God is not mocked. But we cannot see inside his soul to determine how hardened, backslidden, or deceived he may be.

For that reason I find it more useful to focus the discussion on the Bible instead of on the spiritual state of the person I am arguing with. No matter how proud, confident, or loved by God a person is, he can be walking in darkness without knowing it. That is exactly why we have an objective standard against which we can judge our actions. "Take heed unto thyself," Paul told Timothy, "and unto the doctrine; continue in them: for in doing this thou shalt both save thyself, and them that hear thee" (1 Timothy 4:16).

Saying "I'm Christian and gay" proves nothing. The question shouldn't be, *Can a person be homosexual and still belong to God?* but rather, *Is homosexuality right or wrong according to God's Word?*

General Religious Argument Three: "I attend a gay church where the gifts of the Spirit and the presence of God are manifest. How can that be if homosexuality is wrong?"

When Reverend Sylvia Pennington attended her first gay church, she still believed homosexuality was wrong. But something happened to change her mind: "I became aware of the Holy Spirit's presence hovering around, about and within me. They [gay Christians] were sensing the same Spirit that I sensed and loving God back as I was. They were actually worshipping God. And God was there—undeniably there!"[10]

The presence of God in a gay church convinced Pennington that homosexuality was acceptable to Him. What else could it have meant? If He was there, He must approve.

I recall discussing, with a lesbian friend of mine, my own doubts about the gay Christian movement when I was still a part of it. I had been active with the gay church for at least two years by then, but had never gotten past a certain gnawing at my conscience. I was not convinced, and I told her as much.

"But Joe," she said earnestly, "if we were wrong, God wouldn't be blessing our church with His presence. We wouldn't see people coming forward for altar calls, we wouldn't see the gifts of teaching and preaching manifest themselves, and we wouldn't feel His presence the way we do every Sunday." That helped still my conscience a little, but *only* a little. And only for a little while.

Response: This argument is misleading in that it assumes that God's gifts and presence are an indication of His approval.

By Reverend Pennington's description of a gay church, we can assume one of three things: Either God's presence was not there at all, and what she felt was just emotion; or what she (and the others) felt was a demonic counterfeit; or, in fact, God's presence *was* there.

I find it useless to argue over whether or not the presence of God can actually be found in gay churches. Instead, it's best to ask, "So what?" Even if God *is* present in gay churches, and if His gifts *are* manifest there, does that prove He condones homosexuality?

Not at all. God's presence, wonderful as it is, and His gifts, valuable as they are, are given freely. They are neither a reward for, nor evidence of, righteousness. (Please note: I am not arguing that God *is* present in gay churches; I am only saying that, like the "I'm gay and Christian" argument, it is best to stick to the bottom-line issue: *Is homosexuality right or wrong?*)

To illustrate this, consider the Corinthian church. No one could doubt they were genuine believers. Paul opened his letter to them addressing them as "sanctified in Christ Jesus" (1 Corinthians 1:2).

Further, the gifts of the Spirit—teaching, preaching, prophetic words, and so forth—were manifest there. Paul spent all of chapters 12 and 14 teaching them how to manage these gifts. So, God's presence and His gifts were clearly a part of the Corinthian church's life.

And the Corinthian church was a mess. They were, by Paul's own account, carnal and full of divisions (1 Corinthians 3:3-4). Incest was openly committed among them (5:1-5). They were hauling each other to court over lawsuits (6:1-3). And they were getting drunk at the communion table (11:21).

Yet God's presence was at Corinth. Because He approved of their behavior? Of course not. But His gifts and calling, as Paul said in Romans 11:29, are "without repentance." He would not remove them, even when the church was in serious error.

Modern examples abound. By now we have all heard of evangelists or preachers whose ministries thrived even when, unfortunately, they were involved in sexual immorality. For years, in some cases, God's presence and blessing was on their ministry efforts, even as they continued their secret sin. Yet none of us would assume that God approved of their behavior.

What, then, *can* we assume? Two things: First, if God has given someone a gift of the Spirit, that gift may continue to operate even if the person is willfully sinning. Second, the gift, or God's presence, is a sign of grace, not approval. It cannot be said that because the gifts are operating in a church, all the church's activities are legitimate. Legitimacy is determined by Scripture, not spiritual dynamics.

General Religious Argument Four: "My lover and I are in a monogamous relationship, and we truly love each other. That can't be wrong!"

As the gay rights and gay Christian movements have evolved, increasing emphasis has been put on the quality of homosexual relationships. Initially, gay apologists argued for sexual freedom. Today, they argue for legitimacy. As this book is being written, in fact, the nation is holding its breath to see how the Hawaii Supreme Court will rule on the legality of gay marriages.

"God is ecstatic that I'm so happy in a relationship with a woman," a lesbian member of the Metropolitan Community Church gushed on a recent news program.[11] A stable relationship, then, is viewed as evidence of God's blessing. And if true love is involved, so the argument goes, it must be right.

Response: This argument is misleading in that it assumes that love sanctifies a relationship.

It is hard these days to say that love is not the final standard for right and wrong. Love is *nice*, after all; in our culture, it's been nearly deified as something so intense and beautiful, it justifies almost anything done in its name. And with all the hatred and violence in the world, why knock a loving relationship between any two people?

Because love, in itself, does not make a relationship right. In fact, contrary to the "touchy-feely" wisdom of the times, love is not always such a good thing.

An essay on homosexuality and ethics puts it well: "One of the most popular errors in the realm of Christian ethics has been the effort to make love an omnipotent spiritual quality which has the power to sanctify anything that is done in its name."[12]

Love can, according to Jesus, interfere with God's plan for an individual. In Matthew 10:37, for example, He warns His followers that love for anyone, no matter how legitimate the relationship is, becomes sin when it surpasses our love for Him. We can learn an important lesson from King Solomon in this regard. Solomon loved his foreign wives. The problem was, they turned his heart away from God (1 Kings 11:3-4). In his case, love became a snare.

Love is not enough to justify a relationship. An unmarried Christian couple may be very much in love; if they become sexually involved before marriage, it will still be fornication, no matter how much love went into it. And it will *still* be wrong. A married man can fall deeply in love with a woman other than his wife; that will never sanctify adultery.

Likewise two men, or women, may be in love. Their love may run very deep, and they may pledge fidelity to each other and live as happily as any married heterosexual couple. But again, that will not, in itself, justify a homosexual relationship. Scripture places boundaries on human relationships, offering no compromise, even if love is present. If a form of sexual relating is wrong, it remains wrong no matter what degree of love goes along with it.

Or, as a brassy lady once put it, *What's love got to do with it?*

General Religious Argument Five: "I tried to change but I couldn't. God must therefore want me gay."

Of all the subjects related to homosexuality and Christianity, the most heated center on whether or not homosexuals can really change. "I spent 25 years trying to be an 'ex-gay,'" Mel White complains. "I spent tens of thousands of dollars on Christian therapy—I was counseled, exorcised, electric shocked, medicated, and prayed for by the saints."[13]

It's a declaration heard time and again: "I tried not to be homosexual, but I remained sexually attracted to my own gender. Therefore, God intended me to be gay."

Response: This argument is illogical in that it assumes that "unchangeable" and "legitimate" are one and the same.

Whether or not they mean to, religious gays skirt the issue by focusing on whether or not they could change. The priority, to a Christian, should always be whether or not a thing is right *in itself,* regardless of how able or unable a person may be to stop wanting that thing.

The "change" issue comes up in virtually all gay Christian arguments. Mel White repeats it endlessly throughout his book; Roger Biery and Virginia Mollenkott highlight it; Troy Perry does the same. But in recent years, even since these books were published, it's taken on an acrimonious tone.

When the PBS special "One Nation Under God" aired in 1994, for example, viewers across the country heard the testimonies of homosexual men and women who, like White, had attempted to change, were unable to, and now debunked the idea of anyone converting from homosexuality to heterosexuality. But they, like so many in the gay Christian movement, sidestepped the larger issue: *is homosexuality right or wrong?*

It was clear that these gays, most of whom called themselves Christians, had changed their views on homosexuality. At one time, they had believed it was wrong; for some reason, at some point, they decided it was right. Did they change their views on homosexuality because they were unable to overcome it, or because, after carefully studying Scripture and praying for truth, they came to believe homosexuality was as legitimate as heterosexuality?

Based on their own stories—which repeated White's theme of trying to change and being unable to—I have always suspected it was the former. And that says something about their concept of obedience.

"I didn't come for counseling to be made straight," explains Bob Davies, the executive director of Exodus International (a national coalition of ministries helping people overcome homosexuality). "I prayed on my goals, and realized God wanted me to become the most mature, godly man I could be. I'd already decided not to pursue homosexual relationships. Love In Action [the ministry he sought out for help] did not convince me to 'go straight'; they just supported me in my decision." That is where any Christian's concern ought to be: "How can I obey?" rather than "Can I change or not?"

In fairness, the struggle many Christians go through over homosexuality is intense. Depending on how deeply ingrained the homosexual response has become, a person can spend years, perhaps a lifetime, resisting same-sex temptations. It is no wonder so many have given up; I've often said it is a miracle that more of them *haven't.*

But no matter how hard the struggle, God's standards are unchanged. We can't revise them just because we get tired of trying to live up to them.

In responding to this argument, I have found the following thoughts to be helpful:

• *Homosexuals can and do change.* Some change completely, some significantly, others in their behavior more than their inward attractions. It is wrong—and arrogant—for anyone to assume that everyone else's experience will be just like theirs.

Religious gays err when they insist that, because they did not change, no one else will. They are in no position to speak for everyone else. Likewise, men and women who have shifted from a homosexual to heterosexual orientation should never say that just because they so completely changed, everyone else who "really tries" will get the same results. Counseling men and women struggling with homosexuality has taught me to respect the individuality of each person's experience; every case is unique.[14]

• *Homosexual behavior is a sin to be repented of, not a sexual response to be changed.* The difference is crucial. All of us are able, by God's grace, to repent of and resist any given sin. We are not responsible for whatever degree we're still tempted toward that sin.

• *"Unchangeable" and "legitimate" are two very different concepts.* Nowhere in the Bible do we find a sin allowed if the person committing it was unable to get over his desire to indulge it. Certainly homosexuality is a difficult sin to wrestle with—all the more so because wrestling with it is a lonely contest. But resisting sin, no matter how difficult or how weary we grow resisting it, is better than taking it upon ourselves to decide that it isn't a sin. Pat Robertson put it well when writing to Mel White: "My friend, I can't change the Bible. God's Word is forever settled in heaven, and all I can do in my own imperfect way is to do what it says."[15]

• *"Unchangeable" does not mean "acceptable."* I often hear the argument, "I know so many gay people who tried to change, then finally gave up, and are now openly gay and happy." The majority of homosexuals trying to "go straight," they say, never really change and eventually go back into the gay lifestyle.

If that's intended to sway my view, it fails. It reaffirms, in fact, my belief in the wrongness of homosexuality, and in the need for ministry to homosexuals wanting to change.

Why? Because "majority experience" is a poor basis for a Christian argument. The majority, in matters of godliness, is usually wrong.

In general, things tend to move toward a state of decay. That goes for people as well; most who set out on a course to improve their lives are often unwilling to complete it. The Bible proves this out. Most of Jesus' original disciples left Him when His teaching got too intense (John 6:66); the majority of His remaining disciples fled when He was arrested; most of Paul's coworkers abandoned him toward the end of his life (2 Timothy 4:16); and the majority of the churches addressed in the Book of Revelation had serious problems that required repentance. Viewed this way, one might conclude that it is best to see what the majority does, then go and do differently!

At any rate, ethics cannot be determined by convenience. What is wrong is wrong, no matter how deeply ingrained; what is right is right, no matter how difficult. Any attempt to get around these two immutable points is, in the end, futile.

The general religious arguments have a nice tone to them. Like the quaint sayings, "God helps those who help themselves," "All roads lead to God," and "It doesn't matter which religion you choose as long as you're sincere" (none of which are biblical), they're religious enough to sound good, yet unscriptural enough to be dead wrong.

Let's Talk About
Pro-Gay Religious Arguments

(A Sample Dialogue)

Gay Christian Advocate: "How come you're so against homosexuality? Jesus didn't say a word against it."

Response: "I'm no more against homosexuality than any other sin. And, frankly, whether or not Jesus mentioned it doesn't matter. It's plainly condemned in other Scriptures."

Gay Christian Argument: "But His teachings are the foundation of the faith!"

Response: "Not exclusively. Paul said *all* Scripture— that means the whole Bible—is profitable for instruction in righteousness. Christ's teachings are very important, sure. But they're not meant to be our only source of guidance. If that were the case, we wouldn't need a 66-book Bible; we'd just use the four Gospels. But there's plenty of important doctrinal and historical information in the other books, as well. They carry as much weight as the Gospels."

Gay Christian Argument: "Still, if Jesus thought homosexuality was important, don't you think it's strange He said nothing about it?"

Response: "Who is to say He didn't? He might have said quite a bit on the subject and it never got recorded. But even if He didn't, that's no proof it wasn't important to Him. He didn't explicitly say anything in the Gospels about wife-beating or child abuse either, but I'm sure they were important to Him."

Gay Christian Argument: "Wrong! He held up a standard of love for children and respect for women, so it's obvious He did not approve of abusing them."

Response: "Exactly. He also held up a standard for sexual relationships when He referred to the marriage of a man and woman as being God's intention. So even if He didn't say anything about homosexuality, it's obvious He didn't approve of it, just as He didn't approve of anything short of God's intention for the sexual experience which, He clearly said, was marriage."

Gay Christian Argument: "That's an argument from silence."

Response: "So is yours. You see? You can't prove Jesus condoned something just because He didn't mention it. I can't prove what He said or didn't say about it, either. But I do know what He upheld as a standard, and it certainly wasn't homosexuality."

Gay Christian Argument: "Then how do you explain *me*? I'm born again and I'm gay, and I take my Christian life just as seriously as you do!"

Response: "Are you saying whatever a Christian does is okay because he's a Christian?"

Gay Christian Argument: "Of course not, but I know God loves me just as I am."

Response: "Sure He does. But that doesn't mean He approves of every part of your life."

Gay Christian Argument: "He hasn't told me that!"

Response: "What's to tell? We've got His Word in writing. And no matter how much He loves and accepts you, if His Word says your behavior is wrong, then He's already told you what He thinks of it."

Gay Christian Argument: "But if He thinks badly of it, why do I feel His presence every week at my church? Our whole congregation is gay, and He knows it. So why is He blessing us?"

Response: "I'm not sure that He is. We can some-times *think* we're feeling God's blessings, when in fact we're having an emotional, or even a demonic, experi-ence. But just for the sake of argument, let's say you're right—God's presence is in your church. God's presence isn't quite the same as His approval. I can think of lots of ministers who had God's blessing on their lives, but who weren't living right."

Gay Christian Argument: "If you're talking about my being gay, there's no reason He wouldn't condone what I do. I'm in a long-term relationship. My lover and I care very much about each other. God doesn't have any problem with that."

Response: "Because you love each other? That's a shaky foundation. The Bible doesn't say any kind of re-lationship is okay if there's love in it. What about adul-tery? Or fornication? Are those okay, too, as long as both people involved love each other?"

Gay Christian Argument: "You don't understand. People involved in adultery have a choice. I don't! I've been gay ever since I can remember, and I've tried to change more times than I can count. So I've finally ac-cepted who I am, and I'm sure it's okay with Him."

Response: "Because it's okay with you?"

Gay Christian Argument: "Not just me. Plenty of other gay Christians, too! We tried to change because people like you tell us we're sinners, but we don't have a choice over our sexual orientation. I've known so many people who tried to go straight, and all of them are back in the gay community now."

Response: "That doesn't make it right. I know it's hard to change. I know some Christians who have to resist homosexual temptations nearly every day.

"But then, doesn't every Christian have to resist temptations every day? That's what sanctification is all about—growing daily to become more like Him! When we're born again, our sinful feelings don't just vanish. Some of them, in fact, stay with us our whole lives.

"And I know, in your case, those feelings are very deeply ingrained. It would probably be harder for you to resist them than anyone in the church realizes. But God isn't going to change His standards to accommodate ours. Please, don't decide something is right just because it's hard to get over. That's tampering with the Word of God. I think you'll find it's better, in the long run, to obey God's Word than to try to change it."

10

The Nature and Use of the Bible

"The Christian homosexual position when carefully examined can be exposed for what it is at its very core: an attack upon the integrity, sufficiency, and authority of Scripture, which for the Christian church is an attack upon the very nature of our Holy God."

— "Issues in Sexual Ethics,"
United Church of Christ, 1979

Even the most vocal critics of conservative Christians, televangelists, and the "Religious Right" adhere to an unspoken rule: It's not kosher to directly attack Jesus Christ or the Bible. Seldom if ever will a mainstream journalist say, "Jesus was a kook," or "the Bible is hogwash!" Instead, modern attacks on the person of Christ and Scripture come in the form of revisions instead of direct thrusts.

So, the Jesus portrayed in the 1990s is often a socially conscious pacifist or a nonjudgmental rebel; He speaks of love and peace, but never of eternal damnation, self-denial, or of Himself being the *only* way to God

171

172 A Strong Delusion

(as the original Jesus did). He is too nice for that sort of thing.

"If Jesus were alive, He'd be marching here with us!" a well-known actress once said during a gay pride rally, feeling free to interpret the actions of someone she didn't even profess to believe in.

Another example of the "new" Jesus hit me full force when I finished speaking at a recent church conference. "You should be ashamed of yourself for calling homosexuality a sin!" a furious gay man huffed, charging down the aisle toward me. "Jesus never called people sinners, and He never judged anyone!"

Jesus WHO? I wondered as he stomped away. Certainly not the Jesus of the Bible, who was unsparing when denouncing sin, and not at all shy about pronouncing judgment (Matthew 23:13-39).

Likewise, the Bible of the 90s is a good book, but not to be taken as a literal guide for life. Instead of saying they outright reject its teachings, modern critics just diminish its authority. Respect for the Bible is so deeply ingrained in our culture that no one wants to denigrate it; instead, they settle for revisions.

I found this to be true in the gay Christian movement, as well. We had too deep a respect for the Bible to ignore it. But, in my opinion, we weren't willing to obey it, either. Revision was the next best thing.

The pro-gay theology's scriptural arguments, then, are basic revisions of the biblical texts traditionally understood to forbid homosexuality. (I borrow the term "revision" from Stanton Jones, who refers to pro-gay theology as "revisionist" in his excellent article, "The Loving Opposition."[1]) While showing a measure of respect to the Bible, gay Christians generally negate its *authority* or its *sufficiency,* or they claim it has been mistranslated, and thus misunderstood, in modern times.

"The Bible Is a Good Book, But . . ."

(Arguments Diminishing the Authority and Sufficiency of Scripture)

While claiming the Bible is divinely inspired, the pro-gay theology also offers five ways to diminish its authority and/or sufficiency.

Argument One: "The Bible is a good book, but its authors knew nothing of the homosexual orientation when they condemned homosexual behavior."

"The idea of a lifelong homosexual orientation or 'condition' is never mentioned in the Bible," Scanzoni and Mollenkott point out. "The Bible writers assumed that everyone was heterosexual."[2] Roger Biery agrees: "The concept of sexual orientation did not exist in biblical times."[3] Mel White echoes the belief, arguing that the authors of biblical passages against homosexuality "knew nothing of sexual orientation."[4]

Thus Scripture, uninformed about "sexual orientation," is an insufficient guide on sexual matters. "The Scriptures are not self-interpreting," a liberal spokesman insists. "You have to make judgments about how to use today what was written long ago."[5]

Baptist minister George Williamson, pastor of the First Baptist Church of Granville, Ohio, is even more specific when he declares the Bible to be virtually irrelevant to the subject of homosexuality: "We're taking the old book and applying it to the new world in which gay and lesbian people have found themselves."[6]

Response: This argument is *misleading* in that it assumes that orientation justifies behavior.

It is audacious to assume that a behavior is legitimate just because a person is naturally inclined toward it. As shown earlier, recent studies indicate that there may well be such a thing as an "orientation" toward drunkenness and violence (see "Social Justice Arguments—Part One"). So are we to assume, since the biblical authors knew nothing of these orientations either, that we should revise our view of alcoholism or violent behavior?

Nowhere in the Bible is any behavior condemned with a qualification (as in, "Thou shalt not do this thing unless thou hast an orientation toward it"). Nor does the context of a "loving relationship" justify any sexual sin mentioned in Scripture, as pro-gay spokesmen would have us believe. The love between two homosexuals cannot make homosexuality normal or legitimate, any more than the love of two people committing adultery justifies the breaking of marital vows.

Besides, if orientation justifies sexual behavior, why stop at homosexuality? Pedophilia, as mentioned in chapter 2, is believed by some experts to be an orientation; bestiality may be seen the same way in the future. Does biblical ignorance of these conditions nullify biblical injunctions against the actions they result in?

Not if Scripture is truly inspired. If the Holy Spirit indeed moved the biblical authors to write under His guidance, as 2 Timothy 3:16 asserts, then it is insulting to think the third person of the Trinity was ignorant of the human condition. Joseph Gudel, writing in the *Christian Research Journal*, underscores the point:

> It is ludicrous to believe that the Creator of the universe, in guiding the biblical authors, was ignorant concerning the things we now know about homosexuality through modern biology, psychology, sociology, and so forth. To deny scriptural statements about homosexuality on these grounds is to completely deny God's superintendence in the authorship of Scripture.[7]

If the Bible prohibits certain behaviors only because its authors were ignorant of the "orientations" leading to them, then it is not, as it claims to be, "profitable for doctrine, for reproof, for correction, for instruction in righteousness" (2 Timothy 3:16). Rather, it is outdated, uninformed, and irrelevant. There is no middle ground.

Arument Two: "The Bible is a good book, but it has been used in the past to justify bigotry."

Troy Perry likes to remind us of early American believers who used the Bible to justify slavery.[8] Ramey and Mollenkott refer to the Nazi use of Scripture to legitimize anti-Semitism.[9] By comparing the past abuses of Scripture to today's objections to homosexuality, they place the homosexual in the same category as the persecuted, and the conservative Christian in the role of the bigot. "The church was wrong in the past," they seem to say. "Therefore, you must be wrong in the present when you condemn us."

Response: To have been wrong in the past is not proof one is wrong in the present.

There is no question that the church has blood on her hands. Her past errors have been many and, at times, horrendous (examples include, the Inquisition, the Crusades, and the Salem witch hunts). But common sense tells us that past errors are not proof of errors in the present. They *are* proof that we are fallible; we can, if we ignore our past mistakes, repeat sins of prejudice or mistreatment. But Christians cannot be assumed to be committing these errors *now* simply because some committed them *before*.

Additionally, there is a difference between calling a behavior sinful and calling for the persecution of a group of fellow citizens. A conservative stand against gay rights cannot be compared with the Inquisition or the Holocaust. Conservative Christians are not calling for the imprisonment or death of homosexuals; we do not wish them to be denied the right to vote or hold citizenship. In fact, we are against their mistreatment in any form.[10]

There is a clear difference between taking a moral stand on an issue and calling for the mistreatment of people you disagree with. To suggest the two are the same is misleading and unfair.

Arument Three: "The Bible is a good book, but its original language cannot be understood by the average layman. It takes an expert to understand what the authors said about homosexuality."

This argument casts doubt on the average person's ability to comprehend the Bible. More to the point, it suggests an inability to take a stand on biblical issues. After all, if we can't be certain what the Bible's authors meant when they referred to homosexuality, how can we take a stand against pro-gay theology and legislation?

"Normally, it is impossible to understand the meaning of a passage by merely reading it," Roger Biery warns us.[11] "The passage of thousands of years obscures, sometimes beyond recovery, the exact meanings of words," adds John Boswell.[12]

Oddly enough, this inability to understand the Bible seems only to apply to references to homosexuality. Read virtually any gay Christian material and you will find the generous use of other Scriptures with nary a concern for their original Greek or Hebrew meaning. But on the subject of same-sex contact they show a deep, sudden concern for historical, linguistic, or contextual accuracy. Yet, as Elodie Ballentine points out, this argument "fails to account for the fact that the Bible has not been translated by modern English speakers with little knowledge of classical languages."[13]

Indeed, browse through the list of contributors to *The New International Dictionary of New Testament Theology* and *The Theological Wordbook of the Old Testament* (two of hundreds of possible examples) and you'll find innumerable credentials equal to (at the very least) those of the pro-gay theorists. In other words, when comparing the experts who take the conservative view with their liberal counterparts, no one could deny they are at the very least on equal footing.

And that's a generous statement; too generous, I'm sure. First, there aren't that many notable scholars who have taken the pro-gay biblical view. Compared to the hundreds maintaining the traditional position, the pro-gay theology can claim John Boswell, Derek Bailey, Robin Scroogs, L. William Countryman, Victor Paul Furnish, Norman Pittenger, and Helmut Thielicke as its heaviest hitters. Even there, the credentials and standards of some of these heavy hitters can be called into question. Boswell, for example, is a gay historian, not a biblical scholar. Scroogs is a professor at Union Theological Seminary, widely regarded as a liberal institution not holding a high view of Scripture.[14] Countryman allows for prostitution, incest, and bestiality;[15] Thielicke bases his acceptance of homosexuality not on Scripture, but on its allegedly "incurable" nature, jump-starting it from an "ailment" to a "predisposition" to a "talent to be invested."[16]

In fairness, certain portions of the Bible *are* difficult; laymen and experts wrestle with some passages. But it takes neither a rocket scientist nor a scholar to grasp the meaning of most Bible verses. To cast doubt on one area of its translation without scrutinizing the rest of it in a similar manner is inconsistent; it must be taken as a whole, or not at all.

Argument Four: "The Bible is a good book, but conservative Christians pick and choose which of its verses they take literally."

Troy Perry describes an encounter he had with a Bible-quoting woman:

> She said, "Young man, do you know what the Book of Leviticus says?"
>
> I told her, "I sure do! It says that it's a sin for a woman to wear a red dress, for a man to wear a cotton shirt and woolen pants at the same time, for anyone to eat shrimp, oysters, or lobster—or your steak too rare."
>
> She said, "That's not what I mean."
>
> I said, "I know that's not what you mean, honey, but you forgot all those other dreadful

sins, too, that are in the same book of the Bible."[17]

The point is clear—quoting verses against homosexuality is like picking and choosing which Scriptures to stand by and which ones to ignore. Elsewhere Perry expresses it even more strongly: "To condemn homosexuals, many denominations have intentionally misread and misinterpreted their Bibles to please their own personal preferences, remembering only Scriptures that suit themselves, forgetting or ignoring many other Scriptures."[18]

In short, quoting Scripture against homosexuality is a form of inconsistency—hypocrisy, even—since other Scriptures are not taken literally.

Response: This argument is misleading in that it assumes prejudice is the only reason for the conservative position.

A commonsense approach to the Bible shows that certain ceremonial and dietary laws in the Old Testament, such as those quoted by Perry, aren't necessary to follow today. Christians are not, thankfully, under the Mosaic Law (Galatians 3:17-25). But the biblical commandments against homosexual conduct do not appear in the same sections as the dietary and ceremonial laws; in Leviticus (the book Perry's argument centered on) they appear alongside other sexual sins forbidden in both the Old and New Testaments (Leviticus 18:22; 20:13).

Besides, if Perry is to be believed when he says we (conservatives) pick and choose which Scriptures suit us, "forgetting or ignoring" those that do not, an obvious question arises: Why do heterosexual conservatives still preach against heterosexual sins? Why don't we just ignore all references to heterosexual lust, adultery, and fornication? For that matter, why do we still preach against lying and stealing, since we are all, to some degree, tempted toward those sins?

Listen to any conservative preacher who stands against homosexuality, and you will also hear him standing against heterosexual sins. So if we're indeed picking and choosing verses according to our personal preferences, why do we insist on choosing Scriptures that so obviously go against our preferences? Why not make it easy on ourselves and choose only the Scriptures condemning *homosexual* sins, while ignoring the ones condemning *heterosexual* sins?

The fact is, we aren't picking and choosing to suit our prejudice. Our scriptural position on homosexuality is based not on one or two obscure verses yanked out of context. Rather, it is drawn from five specific verses— two found in the Old Testament and three in the New—as well as a general overview of the only form of sexual expression consistently commended throughout Scripture: heterosexual union.

Argument Five: "The Bible is a good book, but its verses are used to clobber gays and lesbians."

"Clobber" is a term that White,[19] Scanzoni, and Mollenkott[20] use to describe the way conservatives quote Scriptures on homosexuality. In fact, the five verses that mention same-sex contact are often referred to, in the gay Christian movement, as "the clobber passages." That cleverly puts the person using them in a negative light; he's not just quoting the Bible—he's *clobbering* people with it.

I remember discussing theology with a gay author on a radio program, when a woman called in and quoted some Bible verses against homosexuality.

"Well congratulations, honey," the author sneered. "You've got all the clobber passages down just right."

Of course, that effectively shut down any rational discussion of the Bible. Decent people don't want to clobber anyone; when they know they'll be accused of doing so, they're less likely to speak up. And that, I suspect, is the reason the "clobber" argument is used so effectively.

Response: This argument is *inaccurate* in that it assumes that "quoting" and "clobbering" are the same.

Actually, Bible verses *have* been used to "clobber" people in the past; that is, they've been implemented in harsh, even cruel ways. In Puritan times, for example, if a person was found guilty of gossip, he would be tied onto a chair attached to a long beam. The chair would then be swung out over a lake and, with the person tied to it, dunked underwater for up to a minute. Likewise, if a person missed church services without good reason, he would be placed in wooden stocks or the pillary (a device clamped around head and hands) and left in public to be humiliated. And unwed mothers, during their pregnancies, might find themselves chained in front of the church, where those passing by would throw rotten fruit at them.

What was wrong here? Was it the fact that the church preached against gossip, neglecting fellowship, or sex outside of marriage? Not at all. The problem was the harsh way these Scriptures were being enforced.

So it is with quoting Scripture against homosexuality. There are those who do so in a harsh, unloving manner; there are those who would, given the chance, implement them in an equally harsh way. Both groups are wrong.

But to simply *quote* a Scripture is not to clobber anyone, as gay spokespersons well know. Perry, after all, has no problem using Bible verses to back his complaints against Anita Bryant,[21] while White feels free to use Scripture when criticizing Pat Robertson.[22] When conservatives quote Bible verses against homosexuality it's called clobbering, yet when gays quote Scripture while arguing against conservatives, it's just—well, quoting Scripture.

Let's Talk About Pro-Gay Scriptural Arguments

Pro-Gay Advocate: "Whatever reason you have for objecting to homosexuality, you won't find any of them in the Bible. It's been badly mistranslated; the fact is, it doesn't condemn gays and lesbians the way you think it does."

Response: "I never said it condemns gays and lesbians, any more than it condemns anyone else. The Bible says we've all sinned, and we're all in need of redemption."

Pro-Gay Advocate: "Fine, but I mean it also doesn't condemn loving sexual relationships between men or between women. Those men who wrote the Bible didn't even know what homosexuality was. It's only in the last century that we have come to understand what sexual orientation is. Biblical writers didn't know anything about people who felt they were gay from the time they were young, and who are in lasting, responsible lesbian and gay relationships."

Response: "But there's no contingency in the Bible about homosexuality. It doesn't say, 'Thou shalt not lie with man as with woman, unless that's your orientation.' The biblical authors probably weren't concerned about what caused certain behaviors—they were concerned with the behaviors themselves.

"By the way, it's quite an insult to God and His Word to ignore what the Bible says about homosexuality just because its authors never heard of 'sexual orientation.' They may never have heard about alcoholism, either, but don't you think they knew what they were talking about when they prohibited drunkenness? Orientation, in itself, doesn't justify behavior."

Pro-Gay Advocate: "But the Bible has always been used to back prejudice; haven't you noticed that? The KKK does it, the Nazis did it, and now the Religious Right's doing it to gays and lesbians!"

Response: "So many people use the term 'the Religious Right' nowadays that I'm not even sure what it is. But if you mean conservative Christians, then you're wrong. Sure, bigots have twisted the Bible in the past, but the fact that some Christians were wrong in the past doesn't automatically mean they're wrong in the present. It only means we should be careful before we take a stand on something, and believe me, I am."

Pro-Gay Advocate: "Don't you think Christians of colonial times said the same thing while they bought and sold their slaves?"

Response: "That's a bad comparison. Gays have never been bought and sold in America; you've never been denied the right to vote; there are no Gay and Straight classrooms or drinking fountains; and you've always had the right to hold property and participate in the political process. In fact, you've always had the same rights all Americans have had. The same sure can't be said about African Americans."

Pro-Gay Advocate: "But bigotry is bigotry, no matter who it's directed against."

Response: "You're right about that. But is taking a biblical stand a form of bigotry? I'm saying homosexuality is wrong. I'm not saying homosexuals are less than human and should be treated as such. It's unfair and inaccurate when you confuse a moral position for bigotry."

Pro-Gay Advocate: "But you're way too sure of yourself. You're not a language expert, so how can you be so sure the Bible really does condemn homosexuality? It's written in ancient languages."

Response: "But it's been translated by experts who know more about language than either one of us. Check the credentials of these guys before you write their translations off. They knew what they were doing."

Pro-Gay Advocate: "Maybe so, but you fundamentalists sure do pick and choose what Scriptures you want to believe in. You yank out the passages on gays and say how terrible we all are, but you don't seem half as concerned about other Bible verses."

Response: "That's true, to a point. Sometimes Christians do get more excited about homosexuality than other sins. But they also preach against sins they're guilty of. Face it, if I wanted to pick and choose which Bible verses to take seriously, I'd only choose the ones that applied to your sins, and never mention the ones that apply to mine. But I don't do that; I admit I've got struggles too. Most other fundamentalists do the same."

Pro-Gay Advocate: "But when you quote verses on homosexuality, you clobber us with them!"

Response: "I've heard you quote Scriptures; you don't seem to think you're hitting someone with them just because you're quoting them. When I quote Scriptures on homosexuality, I'm only doing so to back my belief that homosexuality is a sin."

11

Scriptural Arguments

"Biblical authority is not tyranny: We read, reflect—and reconcile ourselves with scripture; but we never simply remake it or reject it—if we affirm its authority."

— Professor Marion L. Soards
"Scripture and Homosexuality"

This part of the pro-gay theology offers what appears to be a series of conservative, fundamentalist responses to conservative, fundamentalist objections. That is, it meets every Bible verse referring to homosexuality head-on, and attempts to explain why each verse is misunderstood today. It is the boldest part of pro-gay theology, and, for many Christians, the most difficult to respond to. That's because these arguments take what is obvious in Scripture and claim to have discovered that it has a different, heretofore hidden meaning.

To illustrate, let's take a fairly straightforward Scripture: "Come unto me, all ye that labor and are heavy

185

laden, and I will give you rest" (Matthew 11:28). The meaning is clear: Jesus invites the weary to come to Him for rest. No need to check the original Greek or review the cultural context; the Scripture is clear.

Now suppose someone tells you that they have done an extensive word study on this verse, and discovered that Jesus was *really* inviting pregnant women to stay at His maternity ward in Nazareth. It seems ridiculous; the context so clearly points to something else. But if you haven't taken the time to study the original Greek in this verse, you can't technically refute the "maternity ward" idea, though common sense tells you it's nonsense.

That's the power of the pro-gay theology. It takes Scriptures we're all familiar with, gives them an entirely new interpretation, backs its claims with well-credentialed scholars, and gives birth to a new sexual ethic. Common sense may reject it, but until it is examined a bit more closely, it is difficult to refute.

Recently it has been examined, with admirable scholarship and clarity, in two books: *Scripture and Homosexuality*, by Marion L. Soards (Westminster John Knox Press, 1995), and *Straight and Narrow?*, by Thomas Schmidt (InterVarsity Press, 1995). Both authors are professors of New Testament studies, and are eminently qualified to rebut the pro-gay theology's claims. Additionally, they provide the historical and philosophical backgrounds necessary for a complete understanding of the issue from both sides.

Instead of trying to duplicate their work, I will try, in this chapter, to synthesize the pro-gay arguments the reader is most likely to encounter, and then provide concise, user-friendly answers to them. Soards and Schmidt should be consulted for more comprehensive argumentation.

To approach this portion of the pro-gay theology, we will review each Scripture verse referring to homosexuality, establish the traditional view of the verse, cite the pro-gay arguments against that view, and offer a response to each.

Creation/Created Intent
(Genesis 1:27-28; 2:18-24)

So God created man in His own image, in the image of God created he him; male and female created he them. And God blessed them, and God said unto them, "Be fruitful, and multiply, and replenish the earth, and subdue it" (Genesis 1:27-28).

And the LORD God said, "It is not good that the man should be alone; I will make him and help meet for him." . . . And Adam said, "This is now bone of my bones, and flesh of my flesh: she shall be called Woman, because she was taken out of Man." Therefore shall a man leave his father and his mother, and shall cleave unto his wife: and they shall be one flesh (Genesis 2:18,23-24).

Traditional View

God's intention for human sexual relationships is limited to heterosexual union between man and woman in marriage.

Pro-Gay Argument

The Genesis account does not *forbid* homosexuality; it simply doesn't refer to it, for obvious reasons. A gay couple could hardly begin the population process. But these verses cannot be seen as a model for all couples. Many heterosexual couples are childless, or unable to have sexual relations. Are they in sin because they do not conform to the Genesis account?

Response One

While it is true that this passage does not "forbid" homosexual relations, it nevertheless provides the primary model for sexuality by which other forms of sexual expression must be judged. Thomas Schmidt puts it well:

> It [Genesis] provides a basis for biblical com-
> mands and for subsequent reflection on the
> part of those who wish to construct a sexual
> ethic to meet changing situations . . . It is ap-
> propriate for us to explore the relevance of bib-
> lical commands about marriage and to
> evaluate modern homosexuality in light of
> Genesis.[1]

Stanton Jones, in regard to creation as a model for sexuality, adds: "The heart of Christian morality is this: God made sexual union for a purpose—the uniting of husband and wife into one flesh in marriage. God uses sexual intercourse, full sexual intimacy, to weld two people together."[2]

Response Two

The male-female union, introduced in Genesis, is the only model of sexual behavior consistently praised in both Old and New Testaments. While other forms of be-havior—polygamy and the use of concubines, for exam-ple—are introduced and even allowed in the Old Testament, a monogamous relation between husband and wife is the standard upheld in Scripture as the ideal. While the phrase "God created Adam and Eve, not Adam and Steve" seems flippant, it is a fair assessment of created intent: whereas heterosexuality is com-mended throughout the Bible, not once is a homosexual relationship mentioned in anything but negative terms.

The Destruction of Sodom
(Genesis 19:4-9)

> But before they [the angels visiting Lot to judge
> the wickedness of Sodom and determine
> whether or not to spare it] lay down, the men
> of the city, even the men of Sodom, compassed
> the house round, both old and young, all the
> people from every quarter. And they called

unto Lot, and said unto him, "Where are the men which came in to thee this night? Bring them out unto us, that we may know them." And Lot went out at the door . . . and said, "I pray you, brethren, do not so wickedly. Behold now, I have two daughters which have not known man . . . do ye to them as is good in your eyes: only unto these men do nothing." . . . And they said, ". . . Now we will deal worse with thee, than with them" (Genesis 19:4-9, insert added).

Traditional Position

The men of Sodom were attempting homosexual contact with Lot's visitors. Sodom was subsequently destroyed for its great wickedness.

Pro-Gay Argument One

Sodom was destroyed because of the inhospitality of its citizens, not because of homosexuality. Both John Boswell and Michael Bailey support this view, basing it on two assumptions: (1) Lot was violating Sodom's custom by entertaining guests without the permission of the city's elders,[3] thus prompting the demand to bring the men out "so we may know them"; and (2) the words, "to know" do not necessarily have a sexual connotation.

The Hebrew word *yada* appears 943 times in the Old Testament. It carries a sexual meaning perhaps ten of those 943 times. The argument, then, is that the men of Sodom had no sexual intentions toward Lot's visitors.

Response

This argument makes no sense in light of Lot's responses. His first response—"Do not so wickedly, my brethren"—could hardly apply to a simple request to "get to know" his guests. His second response is especially telling: He answered their demands by offering his two virgin daughters, another senseless gesture if the men wanted only a social knowledge of his guests. And why, if these men had innocent intentions, was the city destroyed for inhospitality? Whose rudeness was being judged—Lot's, or Sodom's citizens?

This theory raises more questions than it answers. While Boswell and Bailey are correct in pointing out the seriousness of inhospitality in biblical times, inhospitality alone cannot account for the severity of Lot's response to the men, or for the judgment that soon followed.

Pro-Gay Argument Two

Sodom was destroyed for attempted rape, not homosexuality. This argument is more common; it is proposed by Virginia Mollenkott, Troy Perry, and others, and is far more plausible than the "inhospitality" theory.

"Violence—forcing sexual activity upon another—is the real point of this story," Mollenkott asserts.[4] Accordingly, homosexuality had nothing to do with Sodom's destruction. Had the attempted rape been heterosexual in nature, judgment would have fallen just the same. Violence, not homosexuality, was being punished when Sodom fell.

Response

This argument is partially true; the men of Sodom certainly were proposing rape. But for such an event to include "all the men of the city, both young and old," homosexuality must have been commonly practiced. Mollenkott makes a persuasive case for the event being much like a prison rape, or the kind of assault conquering armies would commit against vanquished enemies.[5] But her argument is weakened by Thomas Schmidt's cited evidence in early literature connecting Sodom with more general homosexual practices:

> The second-century BC Testament of the Twelve Patriarchs labels the Sodomites "sexually promiscuous" (Testimony of Benjamin 9:1) and refers to "Sodom, which departed from the order of nature" (Testament of Nephtali 3:4). From the same time period, Jubilees specifies that the Sodomites were "polluting themselves and fornicating in their flesh" (16:5, compare

20:5-6). Both Philo and Josephus plainly name same-sex relations as the characteristic view of Sodom.[6]

Pro-Gay Argument Three

The real sins of Sodom, according to Ezekiel 16:49, were "pride, fullness of bread, and abundance of idleness . . . neither did she strengthen the hand of the poor and needy." These sins have nothing to do with homosexuality.

Response

Again, this argument is partially true. When Sodom was destroyed, homosexuality was only a part—or symptom—of its wickedness. Romans 1 gives a similar illustration, describing the generally corrupt condition of humanity, while citing homosexuality as a symptom of that corruption. But Ezekiel also says of the Sodomites, "And they were haughty, and committed abomination before me." The sexual nature of these "abominations" is suggested in 2 Peter 2:6-7: "And turning the cities of Sodom and Gomorrah into ashes, condemned them to destruction . . . And delivered righteous Lot, who was oppressed by the filthy conduct of the wicked" (NKJV).

In Jude 7 we similarly read, "Likewise, Sodom and Gomorrah and the surrounding cities, which, in the same manner as they, indulged in sexual immorality and pursued unnatural lust, serve as an example by undergoing a punishment" (NRSV).

Dr. Bruce Metzger of Princeton Theological Seminary mentions other references to Sodom's sexual immorality. In 3 Maccabees 2:5 we read of "the people of Sodom who acted arrogantly" and "who were notorious for their vices." Reference is made in Jubilees 16:6 to "the uncleanness of the Sodomites."[7]

The pro-gay interpretation of Sodom's destruction has *some* merit: Homosexual rape was attempted, and the Sodomites were certainly guilty of sins other than homosexuality. But in light of the number of men willing to join in the rape, and the many other references—

both biblical and extrabiblical—to Sodom's sexual sins, it is likely that homosexuality was widely practiced among the Sodomites. It is also likely that the sin for which they are named was one of many reasons judgment finally fell on them.

The Levitical Law

Thou shalt not lie with mankind, as with womankind: it is abomination" (Leviticus 18:22).

If a man also lie with mankind, as he lieth with a woman, both of them have committed an abomination: they shall surely be put to death (Leviticus 20:13).

Traditional Position

Under Levitical law, homosexuality was one of many abominable practices punishable by death.

Pro-Gay Argument

The practices mentioned in these chapters of Leviticus have to do with idolatry, not homosexuality. The Hebrew word for "abomination," according to Boswell, has less to do with something intrinsically evil and more to do with ritual uncleanness.[8] The Metropolitan Community Church's pamphlet, "Homosexuality: Not a Sin, Not a Sickness," makes the same point: The Hebrew word for abomination found in Leviticus "is usually associated with idolatry."[9]

Roger Biery agrees, associating the type of homosexuality forbidden in Leviticus with idolatrous practices. Pro-gay authors refer to the heathen rituals of the Canaanites—rituals including both homosexual and heterosexual prostitution—as reasons God prohibited homosexuality among His people. They contend that homosexuality itself was not the problem, but its association with idolatry and, at times, the way it was practiced as a part of idol worship. In other words, God was not prohibiting the kind of homosexuality we see today; He forbade the sort that incorporated idolatry.

Response One

The prohibitions against homosexuality in Leviticus 18 and 20 appear alongside other sexual sins—adultery and incest, for example—which are forbidden in both the Old and New Testaments, completely apart from the Levitical codes. Scriptural references to these sexual practices, both before and after Leviticus, show God's displeasure with them whether or not any ceremony or idolatry is involved.

Response Two

Despite the UFMCC's contention that the word for abomination *(toevah)* is usually associated with idolatry, it in fact appears in Proverbs 6:16-19 in connection with sins having nothing to do with idolatry or pagan ceremony:

> These six things doth the Lord hate: yea, seven are an *abomination* [*toevah*] unto him: A proud look, a lying tongue, and hands that shed innocent blood, an heart that deviseth wicked imaginations, feet that be swift in running to mischief, A false witness that speaketh lies, and he that soweth discord among brethren.

Idolatry plays no part in these Scriptures; clearly, then, *toevah* is not limited to idolatrous practices.

Response Three

If the practices in these chapters are condemned *only* because of their association with idolatry, then it logically follows that they would be permissible if they were committed apart from idolatry. That would mean incest, adultery, bestiality, and child sacrifice (all of which are listed in these chapters) are only condemned when associated with idolatry; otherwise, they are allowable. No serious reader of these passages could accept such a premise.

Paul on "Natural" and "Unnatural" (Romans 1:26-27)

> For this cause God gave them up unto vile affections: for even their women did change the natural use into that which is against nature: And likewise also the men, leaving the natural use of the woman, burned in their lust one toward another; men with men working that which is unseemly, and receiving in themselves the recompense of their error which was meet. (Romans 1:26-27)

Traditional Position

Paul views homosexuality as a symptom of fallen humanity, describing it as unnatural and unseemly.

Pro-Gay Argument One

Paul is not describing true homosexuals; rather, he is referring to heterosexuals who, as he says, "changed their nature." The real sin here is in changing what is natural *to the individual.* Boswell takes this argument up when he states:

> The persons Paul condemns are manifestly not homosexual: what he derogates are homosexual acts committed by apparently heterosexual persons. The whole point of Romans 1, in fact, is to stigmatize persons who have rejected their calling, gotten off the true path they were once on.[10]

Ramey and Mollenkott agree, saying, "What Paul seems to be emphasizing here is that persons who are heterosexual by nature have not only exchanged the true God for a false one but have also exchanged their ability to relate to the opposite sex by indulging in homosexual behavior that is not natural to them."[11] In short, Paul in Romans 1 describes heterosexuals who have deliberately committed homosexual acts, thus vio-

lating their true nature. Homosexuality, if committed by
true homosexuals, is not a sin.

Response

Paul is not speaking nearly so subjectively in this
passage. There is nothing in his wording to suggest he
even recognized such a thing as a "true" homosexual
versus a "false" one. He simply describes homosexual
behavior as unnatural, *no matter* who it is committed by.

His wording, in fact, is unusually specific. When he
refers to "men" and "women" in these verses, he chooses
the Greek words that most emphasize biology: *arsenes*
and *theleias*. Both words are rarely used in the New Testament; when they do appear, they appear in verses
meant to emphasize the gender of the subject, as in a
male child *(arsenes)*. In this context, Paul is very point-
edly saying that the homosexual behavior committed by
these people was unnatural to them as males and fe-
males *(arsenes* and *theleias*); he is not considering any
such thing as sexual orientation. He is saying, in other
words, that homosexuality is *biologically* unnatural—not
just unnatural to *heterosexuals*, but unnatural to *anyone*.

Additionally, the fact that these men were "burning
in lust" for each other makes it highly unlikely that they
were heterosexuals experimenting with homosexuality.
Their behavior was born of an intense inner desire. Suggesting, as Boswell and Mollenkott do, that these men
were heterosexuals indulging in homosexual behavior
requires mental gymnastics.

Besides, if verses 26 and 27 condemn homosexual
actions committed by people to whom they did *not* come
naturally, but don't apply to people to whom those actions *do* come naturally, then doesn't consistency compel us to also allow the practices that are mentioned in
verses 29 and 30—fornication, backbiting, deceit, and
so forth—so long as the people who commit them are
people to whom they come naturally?

Pro-Gay Argument Two

This Scripture describes people given over to idolatry, not gay Christians who worship the true God. Troy Perry states:

> The homosexual practices cited in Romans 1:24-27 were believed to result from idolatry and are associated with some very serious offenses as noted in Romans 1. Taken in this larger context, it should be obvious that such acts are significantly different than loving, responsible lesbian and gay relationships seen today.[12]

Response

Idolatry certainly plays a major role in Romans 1. Paul begins his writing by describing humanity's rebellion and decision to worship creation rather than the Creator. The pro-gay theorist seizes on this concept to prove that Paul's condemnation of homosexuality does not apply to *him*—he does not worship idols; he is a Christian.

"But," Schmidt cautions, "Paul is not suggesting that a person worships an idol and decides therefore to engage in same-sex relations. Rather, he is suggesting that the general rebellion created the environment for the specific rebellion. A person need not bow before a golden calf to participate in the general human denial of God or to express that denial through specific behaviors."[13]

A commonsense look at the entire chapter bears this out. A number of sins other than homosexuality are mentioned in the same passage: "Fornication, wickedness, covetousness, maliciousness; full of envy, murder, debate, deceit, malignity, whisperers, backbiters, haters of God," and so forth (Romans 1:29-30).

Will the interpretation applied to verses 26-27 also apply to verses 29-30? Any sort of intellectual integrity demands it; if verses 26-27 apply to people who commit homosexual acts in connection with idolatry, and thus homosexual acts are not sinful if *not* committed in connection with idolatry, then the same must apply to verses

29-30 as well. Therefore, we must assume that fornication, wickedness, covetousness, and maliciousness (and so forth) are also condemned by Paul *only* because they were committed by people involved in idolatry; they *are* otherwise permissible.

This, of course, is ridiculous. Like homosexuality, these sins are not just born of idol worship; they are symptomatic of a fallen state. If we are to say homosexuality is legitimate, so long as it's not a result of idol worship, then we also have to say these other sins are legitimate as well, so long as they, too, are not practiced as a result of idolatry.

Paul and *Arsenokoite*
(1 Corinthians 6:9-10; 1 Timothy 1:9-10)

> Know ye not that the unrighteous shall not inherit the kingdom of God? Be not deceived: neither fornicators, nor idolaters, nor adulterers, nor effeminate, nor abusers of themselves with mankind . . . shall inherit the kingdom of God (1 Corinthians 6:9-10).

> Knowing this, the law is not made for a righteous man, but for the lawless and disobedient . . . for whoremongers, for them that defile themselves with mankind (1 Timothy 1:9-10).

Traditional Position

The phrase, "them that defile themselves with mankind," comes from the Greek word *arsenokoite*, meaning "homosexual." Paul is saying that homosexuality is a vice excluding its practitioners from the kingdom of God.

Pro-Gay Argument

Aresnokoite is a word coined by Paul. It never appeared in Greek literature before he used it in these Scriptures; there were, at the time, other words for "homosexual." Had he meant to refer to homosexuality, he would have used one of the words already in existence.

Most likely, Paul in this verse was referring to male prostitution, which was common at the time.

Boswell points out that the word is peculiar to Paul,
suggesting that he did not have homosexuality in mind
when he used it. Prostitution is Boswell's first choice; if
not that, he suggests that Paul was condemning general
immorality. At any rate, the term, according to this argument, refers to some sort of immoral man but not to
a homosexual.

Response

Paul coined 179 terms in the New Testament. The
terms do not, simply because they are original, significantly change the context of the verses they appear in.
Nor is it remarkable that he would have coined this one,
considering that he derived it directly from the Greek
translation of the Hebrew Old Testament, the Septu-
agint:

> "meta **arsenos** ou koimethese koiten gyniakos"
> (Leviticus 18:22)
>
> "hos an koimethe meta **arsenos** koiten gy-
> naikos"
> (Leviticus 20:13)

In other words, when Paul adopted the term *arsenokoite*, he took it directly from the Levitical passages—
in the Greek translation—forbidding homosexual behavior.
The meaning, then, could not be clearer: Though the term
is unique to Paul, it refers specifically to homosexual behavior.

As for the inference that the word applies to male
prostitution, a breakdown of the word shows that it implies nothing of the sort. *Arsane,* as mentioned earlier,
appears few times in the New Testament, always referring to "male." *Koite* appears only twice in the New Testament, and means "bed" or "couch," used in a sexual
connotation:

> "Let us walk honestly . . . not in chambering
> (*koite*)" (Romans 13:13).

"Marriage is honorable . . . and the bed (*koite*) undefiled" (Hebrews 13:4).

The two words combined, as Paul used them, put "male" and "bed" together in a sexual sense. There is no hint of prostitution in the meaning of either of the words combined to make *arsenokoite*.

Examined carefully, the pro-gay theology shows itself to be built on a very shaky foundation. It is, as Elodie Ballentine points out, "a theology of desperation." But understanding its weakness is only part of our task. Learning how to compassionately but firmly confront it—speaking the truth in love—is our next task.

Let's Talk About Pro-Gay Scriptural Arguments

Pro-Gay Advocate: "Exactly which Scriptures do you think condemn homosexuality?"

Response: "Well, Genesis, for example, makes God's intent for sexual relationships pretty clear when it describes the first couple."

Pro-Gay Advocate: "There's nothing about gays in those verses!"

Response: "My point exactly. The story of Adam and Eve doesn't say anything about homosexuality, only heterosexuality. It gives a very clear picture—a standard—of God's intention for men and women. It's the only standard upheld throughout the Bible. And the story of Sodom, later in Genesis, makes a very strong statement."

Pro-Gay Advocate: "But not against homosexuality. The men in Sodom were condemned for trying to rape Lot and his visitors."

Response: "That, among other things. But you've got to admit that homosexuality must have been practiced pretty commonly in Sodom, or all the men of the city wouldn't have tried to participate in the rape. Besides, several other

Scriptures refer to Sodom's sins as being sexual, as well as idolatrous and prideful. Then, of course, there are the two Scriptures in Leviticus."

Pro-Gay Advocate: "But that's the law. Christians aren't under the law."

Response: "No, thank God, we're not. But the chapters that the Levitical prohibitions against homosexuality appear in also contain other sexual sins condemned in both the Old and New Testaments."

Pro-Gay Advocate: "But homosexuality was associated with idol worship back then. That's why God condemned it."

Response: "So if the other sins in those chapters— incest, for example, and adultery—weren't associated with idol worship, then they'd be okay too?"

Pro-Gay Advocate: "Of course not!"

Response: "Then you can't have it both ways. Either all the sins in those chapters were condemned because of their association with idolatry, or none of them were. The same is true of the first chapter of Romans. Paul lists quite a few sins there—homosexuality included. Of course, homosexuality is not the major sin of Romans 1, anymore than it's the main sin in Leviticus. But it's definitely there, condemned and forbidden."

Pro-Gay Advocate: "But the people Paul described in Romans 1 weren't really gay. That's why it was a sin! God didn't want them changing their nature. They were heterosexuals indulging in homosexuality. What made it wrong was the fact that it wasn't natural to them. Otherwise, it would have been fine."

Response: "And what about the gossips, adulterers, and backbiters in Romans 1? Were they, also, people who weren't really gossips, adulterers, or backbiters? It didn't come naturally to them—*that* was the problem? I don't think so. Nothing in Scripture says a certain sexual behavior is a sin unless it somehow comes naturally to you but not the rest of us."

Pro-Gay Advocate: "But I don't think Paul had any idea what it was like to be truly gay."

Response: "Probably not, and I don't think it would have mattered one bit if he did. It's the behavior he condemned, without even considering what factors might have led someone to that behavior in the first place. Later in the New Testament, in 1 Corinthians and 1 Timothy, he lists homosexuality as one of many other sins keeping people away from God."

Pro-Gay Advocate: "But the word he uses for 'homosexuals' in those Scriptures really means 'male prostitutes.'"

Response: "Where did you get that idea?"

Pro-Gay Advocate: "I read it. A Yale historian did a careful word study on Paul, and that's what he found. The word Paul used—the one we usually think of as meaning 'homosexual'—didn't mean homosexual at all."

Response: "Well, it certainly didn't mean 'prostitute.' The word you're talking about is *arsenokoite*. It's a Greek term Paul took directly from the Greek translation of the Old Testament. In fact, it's from the Greek translation of the Leviticus verses which specifically refer to homosexuality, not prostitution. So there's no way Paul could have meant it as anything but a reference to homosexuality. Besides, if you look at the word itself—a compound of the Greek words *arsane*, meaning male, and *koite*, meaning bed or couch, you'll see there's nothing in the word even suggesting prostitution. It's sex between men, not sex for money, that Paul is writing against."

Pro-Gay Advocate: "Well, I still believe the Bible doesn't say anything against my sexuality."

Response: "And you have every right to believe that. But at some point you've got to ask yourself: Do I believe the pro-Gay theology because I really think it's true, or because, despite the majority opinion of Bible scholars as well as a commonsense reading of the Scriptures, I want to believe it? Is it *conviction* we're talking about here, or *convenience*? Only you can answer that."

12

Confronting the Gay Christian Movement

"Have no fellowship with the unfruitful works of darkness, but rather expose them."
— Ephesians 5:11 NKJV

orruption thrives in a fallen world, where so little goes according to God's plan and so much runs in opposition to it. Much as we may enjoy singing the old hymn, "This Is My Father's World," Scripture indicates it is a world wholly at odds with its creator.

When Satan tempted the Lord in the wilderness (Matthew 4:1-11), he showed Him all the kingdoms of the earth, then made an astounding offer: "All these things will I give thee, if thou wilt fall down and worship me" (verse 9).

Jesus refused the offer without challenging the statement. He knew, as did Satan, that in its present state the world runs as Paul said it does—"according to the prince of the power of the air, the spirit that now worketh in the children of disobedience" (Ephesians 2:2).

In such an environment it is no surprise to find sexual sin on display. Paul, in fact, told the Corinthian church that if they wanted to avoid fornicators they would have to leave the world (1 Corinthians 5:9-10). And though it is important to take a moral stand even in this fallen world, it is more important to remember the priority issue—*if people are without Christ, they are dead;* their immorality is secondary. A public stand against their sins should include an invitation to grace and a recognition that their behavior is symptomatic of a larger problem.

Sin among Christians, or groups calling themselves Christians, is another matter. When it is being practiced without remorse, or redefined from a "vice" to a "gift," the church is called to confront it—not just as sin, but as behavior that no one naming the name of Christ should be involved in! Immorality is serious enough in anyone's life; it is doubly serious when practiced by professing believers.

When gays claim that homosexuality is God's gift, and bring that claim into our churches, then confrontation is a mandate for three reasons. First, the church's integrity is compromised when professing Christians misrepresent Christianity.

When people claiming to follow Christ misrepresent Him through heresy or immorality, Christians need to protest. Several years ago an unusually blasphemous movie titled *The Last Temptation of Christ* was released, brutally misrepresenting Jesus. Christians around the country protested; truth was being perverted and passed off as gospel. So it is with the gay Christian movement: its claims pervert the truth about God's intentions, thereby misrepresenting Him. And Christians need to protest. If homosexuals are comfortable with their behavior, that is one matter; when they say it is done with the blessings of Christianity, then the church, *indignantly*, should insist as Paul did, "The Lord knoweth them that are his. And, let everyone that nameth the name of Christ depart from iniquity" (2 Timothy 2:19).

Second, confrontation is necessary because the gay Christian movement asks us to confirm its members in their sin, when we are biblically commanded to do just the opposite. As Christ's ambassadors on earth—His body, if you will—we unfaithfully represent Him if a professing believer's ongoing sin has no effect on our relationship with that professing believer. This is, in essence, what Paul told the Thessalonians:

> Now we command you, brethren, in the name of our Lord Jesus Christ, that ye withdraw yourselves from every brother that walketh disorderly, and not after the tradition which he received of us. . . . And if any man obey not our word by this epistle, note that man, and have no company with him, that he may be ashamed. Yet count him not as an enemy, but admonish him as a brother (2 Thessalonians 3:6, 14-15).

Finally, unrepentant sin among believers is like a disease; eventually it will spread and effect the entire body. When Paul heard of a Corinthian church member's incestuous relationship with his stepmother, he ordered the man excommunicated (1 Corinthians 5:1-5), then explained the principle of confrontation and—if necessary—expulsion from the community of believers: "Know ye not that a little leaven leaveneth the whole lump? Purge out therefore the old leaven" (1 Corinthians 5:6-7).

A healthy body purges itself of impurities; the body of Christ cannot afford to do less. Confrontation is messy business. It is unnerving and painful; if it is not, there is probably something wrong with whoever's doing the confronting! And it certainly does not match the "nice" image, mentioned earlier, which so many people have of Christianity.

Yet the first New Testament figure to encourage confrontation among believers was Jesus Himself. "If thy brother trespass against thee," He instructed, "go and tell him his fault" (Matthew 18:15). He then outlined a plan for continued confrontation if the erring brother did not repent: the last step was to haul him in front of the church, and then, if he was still unrepentant, treat him as an outcast (verses 15-19).

This same Jesus, gentle and forgiving, never winked at sin. He expected it to be dealt with among His followers. He still does. Consider His rebuke to the church of Thyatira:

> I have a few things against thee, because thou sufferest that woman Jezebel, which calleth herself a prophetess, to teach and to seduce my servants to commit fornication . . . Behold, I will cast her into a bed, and them that commit adultery with her into great tribulation, except they repent of their deeds (Revelation 2:20-22).

Jesus held the Thyatiran church responsible for allowing false teaching to seduce His people. Let the church stand warned: If the gay Christian movement goes unconfronted, its members won't be the only ones facing His displeasure in the end.

How to Confront

How we confront the gay Christian movement is crucial. Paul's instruction—"Yet count him not as an enemy but admonish him as a brother"—should be kept in mind. The members of the gay Christian movement are not our enemies. They claim Christ as their own. I, for one, am not going to judge whether or not they truly know Him. Most of those I knew personally had a genuine salvation experience before they joined the gay church, and who is to say if, and at what point, they may have lost the salvation they found years earlier?

The pro-gay theology is a strong delusion—a seductive accommodation tailor-made to suit the Christian who struggles against homosexual temptations and is

Confronting the Gay Christian Movement 207

considering a compromise. Some who call themselves gay Christians may be truly deceived into accepting it; others might be in simple rebellion. What compels them to believe a lie, we cannot say. What we *can* say is that they are wrong—dead wrong.

When we confront them and their beliefs, we should do it wisely, understanding our motives and concerns, and expressing them clearly. That is why chapters 1 through 5—explaining why we should be concerned about homosexuality in the church, then outlining the history of the gay rights and gay Christian movements—were included. Confrontation is effective when we understand both *why* we need to confront and the backgrounds of the people we are confronting.

Then we need to begin with ourselves. Jesus warned His disciples, and us, against rebuking without self examination:

> And why beholdest thou the mote that is in thy brother's eye, but considerest not the beam that is in thine own eye? . . . Thou hypocrite first cast out the beam out of thine own eye and then shalt thou see clearly to cast out the mote out of thy brother's eye (Matthew 7:3,5).

It would take unusual arrogance to think that we, the Christian community, can approach the gay Christian movement as righteous folks approaching degenerates. If the major scandals in the body of Christ over the past ten years—scandals involving televangelists, famous preachers, reknowned authors, and internationally acclaimed Christian musicians—have proven anything, it is that the body of Christ is not immune to sexual sin. It is not just the gay Christian movement that is in error; *we* are in error, and seriously, which prompted Cal Thomas to pose the question: "Why should the majority accept something they have not seen fully lived out by those who profess to believe?"[1]

That does not negate our responsibility to confront them, but it cautions us to represent ourselves honestly when we approach them: *as sinners approaching other sinners*, nothing more. Reverend Andrew Aquino of the Columbus Baptist Association expressed this perfectly during a recent interview: "My message to the homosexual is: We love you. Come and struggle with us against sin. Don't give in to it."[2]

"If a man be overtaken in a fault," Paul said, "restore such an one in the spirit of meekness, considering thyself, lest thou also be tempted" (Galatians 6:1). Self-examination and a right attitude are prerequisites to confrontation; without them, our words will ring hollow, or destructive, or both. Before confrontation, then, there should be self-examination and repentance.

There should also be wisdom. Going off half-cocked to the local gay church and shaking our fists at its members won't do much good. Tracking down pro-gay spokesmen and challenging them to public debates usually is not very effective, either. It drains away time and energy better spent elsewhere. A commitment to confront is not enough; we need to plan the time and place for it.

Where and When to Confront

There are two general situations in which you are likely to confront the gay Christian movement: within your church (if your denomination is considering accepting the pro-gay theology) and in the public arena, through debates or the media.

At a more personal level, you may confront it among friends or loved ones. Those confrontations, though, will be more about homosexuality in general than the specifics of the pro-gay theology. If a friend or family member has embraced the pro-gay theology, the arguments used in chapters 7 through 11 will be useful to you. But the larger questions—such as, How do I relate to a gay loved one?—are beyond the scope of this book. An excellent resource in this case would be *Someone I*

Love Is Gay, by Bob Davies and Lori Rentzel (InterVarsity Press, 1996).

Confronting the Gay Christian Movement in the Church

While preparing for this chapter I interviewed pastors from the Anglican, Baptist, Reformed, Catholic, Episcopalian, and Lutheran churches, all of whom are debating (at some level) whether or not to accept the pro-gay theology. I asked each pastor or priest how their denomination got to the point where they could even consider such a thing. Several reasons came up repeatedly.

The Elite Versus the Majority

Each pastor noted that people in high denominational positions—the church hierarchy—are in danger of adopting an ivory tower mentality, keeping them out of touch with grassroots concerns. In an academic, somewhat elite atmosphere, there may be more of a tendency toward liberalism and a "critical" view of Scripture. From their position of authority, they may hand down policies entirely at odds with their congregations' beliefs, creating a tension between the laity and denominational leadership.

Special Committees

Two pastors said their denominations had established, years earlier, committees to study homosexuality. Their intentions seemed right; they hoped to develop more effective ministry to homosexuals. But gays and their supporters, having quite a bit at stake in the denomination's acceptance of homosexuality, often joined the committees while conservatives, less enthused about these projects, did not participate. Naturally the committees were often lopsided, composed of more liberal than conservative members.

Committee members turned, in many cases, to the social sciences for information on homosexuality. Receiving a wealth of pro-gay information, they also adopted the revisionist view of Scripture and came (not surprisingly) to the conclusion that the church should revise its view on homosexuality. The ordination of homosexuals, gay marriages, and a commitment to gay rights were then recommended. At the denomination's general conferences, the committee proposals were voted on (and usually voted *down*) by the more mainstream, conservative members of the denomination; the committee's reports were tabled, to be studied further and voted on again at the next general conference, when the cycle would begin again. (This is, of course, an over-simplification; the details and events have varied in each denomination involved in these discussions.)

In each case, increased lay involvement was recommended by the pastors. "Most people in our churches don't want this!" one said, referring to the pro-gay theology. "But if they don't want it, they'll have to get more involved in their local congregations and do something about this."

A few ideas for getting involved, and confronting the pro-gay theology within denominations, came up in these discussions.

1. *Know your denomination's official position.* If you are not sure what it is, write to the general headquarters of the denomination and request a copy of their position statement on homosexuality and the Bible. In most cases, you will find that your church still officially holds to a conservative position; remind people of that during every discussion you have on the subject. Church authority is still, in most cases, on your side.

2. *Know your pastor's position on homosexuality.* If he takes a pro-gay position, you will naturally have a hard time soliciting his support. But if you are reading this book, it is a safe bet you are under traditional leadership.

Ask your pastor for ideas on combatting the pro-gay theology in your denomination. Explain to him that you are not asking him to do anymore than he is already doing; pastors are swamped, and they do not usually appreciate a congregant asking them to get involved in yet another cause! But tell him you want to get more involved in standing for truth within your church. Ask for his blessing and counsel.

3. *When possible, participate in your denomination's process.* Join committees your denomination has formed to study the issue of homosexuality and the Bible. Use the materials in this and the books listed under "Suggested Reading" (at the end of the book) to bolster your arguments. Be sure to contribute verifiable information proving that homosexuality is not innate, unchangeable, or biblically allowed. Also contribute ideas on how to lovingly minister to homosexuals without compromising the truth.

4. *Invite speakers to address your church.* Ask speakers to your Sunday school classes, midweek services, and main church services on the subject of homosexuality and the Bible. Locate people in your area who take a stand on this issue, and support them. If you do not know of anyone in your area who teaches on the subject, contact Exodus International for referrals. Encourage your church and pastor to consider the need for education on homosexuality; people are perishing for lack of knowledge.

5. *Sponsor seminars on homosexuality.* Seminars are great vehicles for delving into a topic from all angles. A well-balanced seminar on homosexuality will include workshops on gay rights issues, the pro-gay theology, counseling homosexuals, responding when a loved one is gay, and how the church in general can better address homosexuality in America. This is an excellent way to serve and educate the Christian community in your area.

6. *Ask your pastor about developing ministries in your church.* Establish counseling and support groups for people struggling against homosexuality, and for families with homosexual loved ones. (See "Suggested Reading" for materials on starting church ministries to homosexuals.)

Pastor Ken Korver of Southern California proved that any church can do this. Having read some books on homosexuality and feeling a burden to do something constructive about the problem, he invited several speakers to his church for a special seminar on the subject. He then made two announcements to his congregation: First, he said that if anyone in his church struggled with homosexuality, he wanted them to call him personally during the week, and they would begin meeting together weekly, *and privately,* for Bible study, accountability, and encouragement.

He then asked his congregation how many of them would be willing to make themselves available to the people who contacted him during the week wanting help: "Will you be there for them when they're tempted, and will you walk with them through their process of overcoming homosexuality?"

More than 70 people responded. That was five years ago. Pastor Korver's ministry to homosexuals is still thriving. If more churches followed his example, we would be far more effective in combatting gay theology. As the leaders of the conservative Ramsey Colloquium noted,

> One reason for the discomfort of religious leaders in the face of this new [gay] movement is the past and continuing failure to offer supportive and knowledgeable pastoral care to persons coping with the problems of their homosexuality.[3]

We cannot, with integrity, denounce a problem while doing little or nothing to solve it.

Years ago we learned this when combatting abortion. For decades we railed against the crime of killing the unborn. Yet Roe versus Wade passed and the abortion industry thrived. At some point we realized our approach was too limited. It wasn't enough to tell women what *not* to do—we also needed to move alongside them and help them do what was right.

So we established homes for women to carry their children to full term in lieu of abortion. Christian counseling centers for crisis pregnancies cropped up. Support groups for women who'd had abortions became commonplace as well. We became a part of the solution, not just another voice denouncing the problem.

If our churches are going to effectively withstand the gay Christian movement, they will have to do more than argue against it. They will have to become safe havens for women and men struggling against homosexuality— places where these believers, like all others, can freely say, "I struggle; help me." If we fail them when they need our support, we need not be surprised when they abandon biblical ethics altogether and become our most boisterous critics.

Confronting the Pro-Gay Theology in the Public Arena

You may sense a calling to publicly confront this teaching, whether in media interviews or public discussions. I use the word "calling" very literally. Some people are called and gifted by God to public debate, and many (perhaps most) are not. I have found this to be a crucial point. Many people are concerned about this subject. But concern, in itself, does not qualify a person for public speaking. The public arena is a harsh battlefield that no one should enter without calling and preparation. Before venturing into it, seek input and confirmation from your pastor and the people who know you best. Be sure you are commissioned and equipped; better not to go at all if you are uncertain.

Still, the public arena can be a great vehicle for truth. Since 1988 I have participated in an average of 40 radio and television shows per year, both secular and Christian. Not once, even during the most hostile interviews, has the time been wasted. Phone calls, without exception, have always followed from people wanting help. Counseling appointments increased; relationships across the country were established by phone or correspondence. So, speaking in the public arena has proved to be very effective.

The need for Christians taking a stand on this issue is greater than ever. The truth about homosexuality won't be effectively set forth by a mere handful of Christian speakers. We need a variety of men and women, from all backgrounds, speaking to the press, the media, campuses, and professional conventions.

You may be one of them. If so, let me offer a few ideas on effectively confronting the pro-gay theology in the public arena.

1. *Do your homework.* At the risk of sounding repetitious, let me encourage you again to read the books listed in the "Suggested Reading" list at the back of this book. Learn all the Scriptures that refer to homosexuality, and understand the pro-gay interpretations of each. Make sure you have at least one response to each pro-gay interpretation memorized or on-hand.

Also, make sure you are aware of the general arguments the gay Christian movement sets forth (see chapters 7 through 11) and be certain you can articulate a response to each of them, as well.

2. *Do not assume that every opportunity to speak publicly is a calling.* Because there is so much media interest on this subject, once you've spoken publicly on it, you may well find yourself deluged with interview requests, both secular and Christian. A good principle to keep in mind is this: *The need always outweighs the availability.* Opportunity and calling are two different things.

I have learned to turn down almost as many requests for interviews as I accept. Stewardship requires
it; we've got only so much energy to expend, after all.
When invited to a debate or an interview, ask yourself
the following questions:

• Will this be beneficial to the purposes I am trying
to achieve?

• Will I be given enough time during this interview to
make an impact so that it will be worth my time to accept this invitation?

• Am I the best one to do this, or is someone else
available who could do it better?

By making sure each opportunity passes this three
fold test, you'll avoid the burnout that inevitably comes
when people don't wisely monitor their time and activities.

3. *Don't be naive.* If you are going to be a guest on talk
shows, or interviewed for articles or news programs, you
are likely to be working with reporters and moderators
who disagree with you. Some may be downright hostile.
That is the nature of the media environment. Be sure you
are mentally prepared (again, by doing your homework
beforehand) and psychologically prepared as well.

When my friend Sy Rodgers (an extraordinary advocate for balanced ministry to homosexuals) was a guest
on a prominent talk show, the host approached him just
before the show began and greeted him with: "I think you
are offering false hope when you say homosexuals can
change and I'm going to nail you when we get out there."

When Dr. Joseph Nicolosi (a psychologist offering
help to homosexuals desirous of change) spoke to a
school board meeting in San Francisco, he was drowned
out with shouts and catcalls; the school board officials
did nothing to intervene.[4] And when a conservative activist addressed a Northern California church, gay activists surrounded the building, blocking entrances and
vandalizing property. Yet the local media was virtually
silent; had conservatives been staging such a disrup-

tion, there is no question it would have been front-page news.[5]

"The establishment media," Cal Thomas notes, "have developed a relationship with the political objectives of gay rights activism that has shamefully compromised their ability to report objectively and fairly on this issue."[6] A polling of the media in the early 1990s confirms Thomas's complaint: Eighty percent of the newsmen questioned said they did not believe homosexuality was wrong, 90 percent favored abortion rights, and 20 percent attended church or synagogue. A fair interview, under these conditions, is hardly a foregone conclusion.

Yet we can hardly expect the world to celebrate the Christian view. Jesus gave us fair warning: "If ye were of the world, the world would love his own: but because ye are not of the world, but I have chosen you out of the world, therefore the world hateth you" (John 15:19).

When you openly criticize any form of gay ideology, including the pro-gay theology, you are going against the tide. The disapproval of the world cannot be avoided; it is often a confirmation that you are on the right track. (When Ronald Reagan was castigated by the American Civil Liberties Union for proclaiming 1983 the "Year of the Bible," he said he wore their criticism like a badge of honor!) In fact, when I consider the moral and philosophical views of the people throwing their support behind the gay rights and gay Christian movement, I am amazed that "gay Christians" (who should know enough of the Bible to know better) are glad to get their support. If Phil Donahue, Joan Rivers, Cher, and Mae West supported my moral views, I would be gravely concerned.

All media and public work is not, of course, hostile or imbalanced. I have found much of it to be challenging, fruitful, and sometimes downright fun. But it is best to go into it prepared for anything. So take Jesus' advice—be wise as a serpent yet innocent as a dove (Matthew 10:16).

Since others have been publicly speaking on this issue for years, we might as well learn from their mistakes and their triumphs. In my opinion, the following are the most crucial mistakes to avoid, and the best ideas to implement, when confronting the pro-gay theology in the public arena.

What *Doesn't* Work

1. *Do not attack the character of homosexuals.* Some Christians seem bent on proving that homosexuals are neurotic, sex-obsessed, or hateful. (During the Anita Bryant campaign, for instance, one well-known pastor remarked, "Those so-called gay folks would just as soon kill you as look at you!")

This backfires for two reasons. First, it speaks poorly for the person doing the attacking and gains sympathy for the gay viewpoint. "The Church is discredited," a pro-gay author once noted, "occasionally by an inexcusable error of fact, but far more often by some exaggeration or tendentious assertion."[7] Attacking the character of an opponent betrays a weak argument while making the opponent look all the better. "Abuse a man unjustly," Edgar Watson Howe observed, "and you will make friends for him."

Second, this tactic skirts the issue. If homosexuality is wrong, it is wrong whether committed by a scoundrel or a wonderful person. Attacking the character of homosexuals raises an obvious question: Would same-sex contact be all right if the people involved in it were nice people?

If that were the case, then homosexuality would certainly be legitimate. I knew far too many lesbians and gay men who were responsible, likeable, hardworking people; I have known far too many heterosexuals who were outright despicable.

Keep the issues straight. The character of the person is not in question. The person's behavior is.

2. *Do not relay gruesome, explicit "facts" about homosexual sex.* Some Christian speakers feel a need to not only condemn homosexual behavior, but to describe its

more sensational aspects in the most lurid of terms. Instead of just saying sex between men or women is unnatural, they reach for the wildest sexual practices committed by some (definitely not all) in the homosexual community, hold those practices up as the "gay norm," and, like a movie camera zooming in on a bloody corpse, linger over the crude details. This serves no good purpose. In fact, it needlessly alienates us from gays who hear these remarks.

I remember sitting in a gay bar in 1978, where someone had brought in some literature put out by Christians on homosexuality. The pamphlets and fliers, detailing all the elaborate sexual things we allegedly did to each other, was being passed from barstool to barstool. You could tell another man was reading it by the fresh eruption of laughter. *We found these Christian materials hilarious!* They were largely untrue, and obviously designed to incite revulsion toward homosexuals by accusing us of practices most of us had never heard of, much less indulged in.

This backfires for both reasons listed previously: it discredits the speaker, and skirts the larger issue. Homosexuality is wrong, whether committed 5,000 times a year during sadomasochistic rituals, or once in a 50-year monogamous relationship. It is wrong *in and of itself.*

3. *Do not portray gay extremists as examples of all homosexuals.* People see through such tactics. Extremists can be found in any group, Christian and non-Christian alike. To point out the extreme factions of the gay rights movement and hold them up as the norm is just as cheap and manipulative as picking out the "pro-lifers" who shoot abortionists and saying they are representative of the whole pro-life movement. Let's avoid such games.

4. *Do not use cliches.* Cliches are grating. They weaken the argument of the person using them, and they make their user sound as though she or he is relying on sayings rather than sound reasoning. Following are a few cliches to avoid:

• "Gay lifestyle." There is no such thing. Homosexuals live their lives in many ways. Some are militant; many but not all are promiscuous; some are moderate, some conservative. To categorize one lifestyle as the norm for all of them is inaccurate and will cast doubt on other statements you make.

• "We love the sinner but hate the sin." That's true, but let's find another way to say it. This one is almost certain to get a laugh if you use it in public, just because it has been so overused. (Also, I suspect, because it is a bit too simplistic.)

• "If you are gay, that's your choice." It is not. No one *chooses* to be homosexual. People do choose, however, to *act* on their homosexual desires. Make the distinction and keep it clear.

• "God made Adam and Eve, not Adam and Steve." I referred to this one earlier in this book, but I would avoid using it in public. It sounds sarcastic, like a mockery of homosexuals. Sarcasm never wins an argument.

What *Does* Work

1. *Stick to verifiable facts rather than anecdotes or rhetoric.* "The Bible says . . . ," "studies have shown . . . ," "surveys have proven . . . ," are all verifiable and tough to argue against. For example, rather than just saying, "I know homosexuals can change because I did," I prefer saying, "Treatment programs for people like me who wanted to change have certainly been successful," and then I name the programs or studies so the audience can check for themselves (see chapter 7).

2. *Admit error.* I have found it helpful to admit the past mistakes of some Christians, rather than blindly defend everything we've done in the past. We've made mistakes, and if we refuse to admit them, we can hardly expect gays or society to take us seriously.

"We have treated homosexuals horribly in the past," Professor Mouw said in a recent interview with *Christianity Today*. "And if homosexuals today are angry with the church, we first need to repent of our past sins and then try to seek the credibility in this society to begin speaking."[8]

3. *Stay flexible when discussing theories, yet adamant when discussing the Bible.* What the Bible says about homosexuality is absolute, but theories that often come up—such as those on the origins of homosexuality, whether or not homosexuality is changeable, and how the average homosexual lives—are all subject to question. When discussing the Bible we can be adamant; when discussing our theories, more caution is needed.

We can't be certain, for example, what makes people homosexual (theory), yet we *can* be certain that homosexuality is wrong (Scripture). So, although I strongly feel that family dynamics have a lot to do with the development of homosexuality *in most cases*, I'm open to other theories as well, and I say as much when speaking on the subject. Likewise, I am not at all convinced that homosexuality is inborn; when speaking on the subject, I give the same reasons against this view that I list in chapter 7: *The studies are inconclusive at best.* But I'm open to future evidence; that won't change my position on homosexuality one bit. If it is biblically condemned, then how it begins is secondary.

Stay flexible enough to admit that any theory may be wrong, and stick to the facts of Scripture. A discussion of the pro-gay theology should return, again and again, to what the Bible says. That is the bottom line—*don't let yourself get sidetracked!*

4. *Remember that confrontation need not always seem successful in order to have been successful.* We may walk away from a debate, interview, or discussion feeling as though all our points fell flat. Or our denomination may swing toward the pro-gay theology despite

our best efforts. Or a gay friend may ignore all our arguments, no matter how carefully thought out and presented, and still join the gay Christian movement. All of this can leave us feeling as though we have failed.

It is best to remember, when confronting the gay Christian movement, the parable of the sower:

> And when he sowed, some seeds fell by the way side, and the fowls came and devoured them up: Some fell upon stony places, where they had not much earth . . . And some fell among thorns; and the thorns sprung up, and choked them. But other fell into good ground, and brought forth fruit (Matthew 13:4-5, 7-8).

The sower's job was *to sow*. The type of ground the seeds fell on was not his responsibility. If we looked at his work statistically, we might say he was a failure. Most of his seeds did not take root; most of the ground the seeds fell on was hard, or scorched, or thorny. But there were results as well—there always are *some* results, even if they may seem minimal.

We are not called to persuade, but to present. As stewards of truth, our job is to present the truth clearly, lovingly, and responsibly. When standing before the judgment seat of Christ, we will not be asked how many homosexuals we were able to persuade out of the gay Christian movement. But surely we'll be asked how faithfully we stewarded the truth we've been given, and how lovingly yet boldly we presented it.

When asked that question, may it please God that we may answer with confidence, and then hear Him say, "Well done, good and faithful servants."

13

Beyond Delusion

"The trouble with the future is that it usually arrives before we're ready for it."
— Arnold H. Glascow

I t took less than five minutes for me to delude myself into thinking that homosexuality was acceptable to God. It would take another five years before I was willing to reconsider. And my decision to leave the gay community was made as quietly and uneventfully as my decision to enter it had been.

In January of 1984, while channel surfing in my apartment, I ran across an old acquaintance who was being interviewed on Christian television. We had never been close, but I had always admired him. In the early 1970s, he was one of the biggest names in contemporary Christian music. I had met him a few times, and had even worked closely in ministry with his sister, an accomplished singer in her own right. He was a well respected, established leader in the Christian community.

But tonight he was talking about his failures, not his accomplishments. Evidently his marriage had nearly fallen apart, his interests had become worldly, and his heart had hardened. "God basically told me I had to choose between life and death," he said solemnly. "I had no relationship with Him at all."

I was astounded. The details of his life over the past few years were almost sordid! And all this had occurred while he was still active in the ministry. He had recently experienced renewal, and was encouraging Christian audiences toward a closer, more accountable relationship with God and church.

He hadn't gotten involved in homosexuality (or any sexual sin, to my knowledge), but his situation had become nearly as serious as my own. But whereas I had revised my beliefs to suit my problems, he admitted his problems and dealt with them. Now his marriage was restored, his ministry was renewed, and he was clearly back in the saddle. I couldn't help comparing the way I had handled my life to the way he'd handled his. The more I considered it, the more uncomfortable I became.

I switched the television off and sat in silence for nearly an hour, considering the unthinkable. *Could I have been wrong all these years?*

They hadn't been all bad, those years I'd spent in the gay Christian movement. I had good friends, a better than average job, my own apartment, and in many ways a lifestyle typical of any 29-year-old: work, dating, parties, future plans.

But it was time to be honest—I missed what I had abandoned the day I had my first adult homosexual encounter: confidence before God, and the peace that comes with it. I'd been without it for so long, I'd almost forgotten what it was like.

But not quite. I recognized it on my old friend's face—the peace of a man reconciled to God and living humbly before Him. The peace of a clear conscience; the confidence of integrity. I'd sold mine like Esau sold his birthright, and for what? Gratification. A bowl of porridge; nice for the moment, but never enough. And never able to satisfy the longing I'm sure every woman and man has, no matter how stifled it has been, to know God and live in harmony with Him.

I want it back, I began whispering. It was a scary thought—pursuing it could mean putting my life through a complete shakedown—but it refused to leave.

Years earlier I had wanted it all—everything I could grab. Now I'd had it, at the cost of the one thing so easy to give up and so hard to live without.

Now I wanted it back: the peace I used to have, the confidence that I was truly living as God intended. Not just the assurance that He loved me; I'd had that all along and it was not enough. I needed, more than ever, to know I was *right* before Him—right in my beliefs and right in my lifestyle. And so for the first time in years, I reopened the Bible to the verses on homosexuality, and breathed a scary prayer: *I'm finally willing to admit I'm wrong about this. If I am wrong, please show me.*

Within an hour, virtually all the rebuttals to the pro-gay theology I've listed in this book came to me as clearly as though they'd been written in a letter. And with them came a horrifying realization: *For five years of my life I'd been wrong.*

• Wrong when I'd stepped into the aisle, taking communion as a gay Christian, and eventually joining the staff of the Metropolitan Community Church as a pianist, student minister, Bible study teacher, and counselor.

• Wrong when I'd encouraged others to do the same, assuring them that God made them gay, even encouraging them to end their marriages rather than deny their "true" selves.

• Wrong when I'd spoken to college campuses as a "proud, gay Christian," eagerly taking on the students who thought homosexuality was sick, shooting down arguments from well-intentioned but poorly informed Christians.

• And wrong—God help me, so wrong!—in entering into relationship after relationship, trying time and again to form a partnership without ever being honest enough with myself, or the men I was involved with, to admit I wasn't sure homosexuality was right. Not once was I able to sustain a relationship with a man for more than six months, not because the relationship was homosexual, but because of my own deep problems with intimacy—problems I'd never been willing to face—which made it impossible for me to stay with anyone, male or female. (I had tried both, many times.)

I'd had no right to involve anyone in my life under those circumstances; *it* was wrong, *I* was wrong.

I had been wrong for five years, and there was nothing I could do to atone—nothing I could do at all but face it and weep. For the first time in my life I was suicidal; the grief I was experiencing was unbearable, expressed night after night while I thrashed and moaned in bed, visualizing the numbers of people I had hurt and let down, drowning in my own failure.

But godly sorrow works itself into repentance, and I came to realize that repentance in its truest form is not just grief, but a life separated unto God. I began mine by moving. Without a new location, away from old habits and influences, I knew I'd never make it. I joined a Bible-believing church, eventually hooked up with friends I'd known from the ministry years earlier, and healing began—as it always does—slowly and unobtrusively.

Three years later, after intensive therapy and soul searching, I began counseling others who had been in my situation, and was astounded to see how many there were! My work (and my joy) has been in this field—ministry to repentant homosexuals—for eight years now. And during those eight years I have been reminded that if someone as deluded as I was can be brought out of homosexuality, then surely anyone can.

But when they are brought beyond delusion, *who is waiting for them*? Is the church a father to the prodigal, racing to meet him halfway and celebrating his return? Or is the body of Christ better represented by a self-righteous older brother, distant and cold, uninvolved? When addressing the problem of homosexuality, these are perhaps the most important questions to consider.

Shortly after my own repentance I read Francis Schaeffer's last book, *The Great Evangelical Disaster* (Crossway Books, 1984). I believe the book to be prophetic, speaking to the most pressing issues facing Christianity today, 12 years after it was written.

While calling for a balance between compassion and conviction, Dr. Schaeffer remarked, "The church is to be a loving church in a dying culture."[1] And by that standard, I'm afraid, the church is nowhere near what it needs to be. Our hearts seem unequipped to confront the gay Christian movement, even as it grows by leaps and bounds. The future has arrived, and we are unprepared for it.

In fact, by our lack of love, I believe we contribute to the growth and strength of the gay movement. Of course, individuals will answer to God if they embrace error, and "gay Christians" will have a lot to answer for. But what about us? To what extent have we helped them along the way toward a strong delusion?

Perhaps they can best tell us themselves:

> We grow because hundreds of thousands of gay and lesbian Christians who are despised and rejected by the Catholic and Protestant churches of their childhood have no where else to go.
>
> —Mel White[2]

> If the church had really done their missionary work, I don't think that MCC [Metropolitan Community Church] would have ever existed.
>
> — Troy Perry[3]

While the church invokes truth in its stand against the gay Christian movement, as it must, does it also contain enough love—in deeds, not just words—for the members of the movement it stands against? With God as our witness, can we really say we love homosexuals?

Perhaps we can. But if we do, where are our tears? Moses agonized in intercession for his people when they sinned and God's wrath nearly came down on them.

Jesus wept openly over Jerusalem, knowing all it could have been yet foreseeing its doom. Paul's heart-desire was to see the Jews (who at times opposed him violently) saved. But today, who weeps for homosexuals; whose heart cries out to see them brought to the truth?

If someone *is* weeping for them, let me respectfully but plainly say they are doing it awfully quietly.

The top Christian radio and television programs in America regularly feature guests who fight the gay rights movement, and teach others to do the same. That's well and good. Compare, though, the number of guests they feature calling us to *fight* the gays with the number of guests they feature teaching us how to *minister* to them. The imbalance can't help but be noticed.

When I served as president of Exodus International (a national coalition of ministries dedicated to helping repentant homosexuals and their families), I was truly discouraged by the number of major ministries that welcomed, through their support and visibility on their shows, conservative antigay activists, yet had little or no time for us. And while I thank God for conservative activism, I know that, in itself, it only addresses half the problem. And, as mentioned earlier, local churches have been reluctant to tackle the problem, as well.

But hopeful signs abound. Campus Crusade showed considerable boldness when, in October 1995, they placed ads, featuring people who had overcome homosexuality, in campus newspapers across the country. Dr. Beverly LaHaye, though one of the nation's most outspoken opponents of the gay agenda, has consistently shown her support for ministry to homosexuals as well. Indeed, her conferences have traditionally featured speakers from the political *and* the ministerial perspective. And conservative columnist Cal Thomas has always been a friend to those ministering to homosexuals, as well as to those opposing their goals.

Ultimately, though, the church's ability to withstand the gay Christian movement will be determined by our willingness to be inconvenienced. It will be inconvenient to study the gay theology and learn how to refute it. It will certainly be inconvenient to train up Christian spokesmen to stand for truth in our campuses, television studios, and sanctuaries. Establishing ministries in our churches to repentant homosexuals will be inconvenient and controversial. And getting involved with them, through one on one discipling and relating, will no doubt be a major inconvenience as well.

Yet nothing less will stem the tide of pro-gay theology. And should we refuse to be inconvenienced, and let the tide wash over us, for whom but ourselves do we think the bell is going to toll?

I was fortunate. Loving friends took me in when I repented. Strong brothers welcomed me into their fellowship. I was forgiven, accepted, and restored. I could only wish the same for every woman or man who, by God's grace, is also brought beyond delusion. And perhaps, with an awakening to our need for each other no matter what our background or former sins, more prodigals will find a celebration waiting for them when they, too, return to their father's house.

It is not a pipe dream. Episcopal seminarian William Frey envisioned it some time ago, and, as he relates it, it sounds like nothing more than basic Christianity:

> One of the most attractive features of the early Christian communities was their radical sexual ethic and their deep commitment to family values. These things drew many people to them who were disillusioned by the promiscuous excesses of what proved to be a declining culture. Wouldn't it be wonderful for our church to find such countercultural courage today?[4]

Wonderful indeed.

Wonderful, admirable, and—most important—*entirely possible.*

Suggested Reading

The following eight books, in combination, will equip anyone with the breadth of knowledge needed to intelligently discuss the biblical, sociological, and psychological issues related to homosexuality.

Baird, Robert and Baird, M. Katherine. *Homosexuality: Debating the Issues.* Amherst: Prometheus Books, 1995.

Bayer, Ronald. *Homosexuality and American Psychiatry: The Politics of Diagnosis.* New York: Basic Books, 1981.

Dallas, Joe. *Desires in Conflict.* Eugene: Harvest House Publishers, 1991.

Schaeffer, Francis. *The Great Evangelical Disaster.* Westchester: Crossway Books, 1984.

Schmidt, Thomas. *Straight and Narrow?* Downers Grove: InterVarsity Press, 1995.

Soards, Marian. *Scripture and Homosexuality: Biblical Authority and the Church Today.* Westminster: John Knox, 1995.

Wood, Gwen and Dietrich, Jon. *The AIDS Epidemic: Balancing Compassion and Justice.* Portland: Multnomah Press, 1990.

Resources

Educational materials by Joe Dallas on homosexuality and related issues are available through Genesis Counseling. For a free catalogue of the Genesis Audio and Video Cassette Series, and for information on seminars by Joe Dallas, please contact:

Genesis Counseling
1774 North Glassell
Orange, CA 92680
(714) 502-1463

Notes

Introduction

1. In my title I've put the term *gay Christian movement* in quotes to clarify my belief, at the start, that "gay" and "Christian" do not go together. By now, though, I'm sure the reader knows my position, so there is no need to repeat the quotation marks each time I use the term.

2. From Levi's speech to the National Press Club during the 1987 Washington Rally; cited in William Dannemeyer, *Shadow in the Land* (San Francisco: Ignatious Press, 1989), p. 86.

3. Mel White, *Stranger at the Gate* (New York: Simon and Schuster, 1994), p. 311.

4. Troy Perry, *The Lord Is My Shepherd and He Knows I'm Gay* (Los Angeles: Nash Publishing, 1972), p. 3.

5. Malcom Boyd, *Gay Priest* (New York: St. Martin's Press, 1986), p. 2.

6. White, p. 6.

7. Philip Yancey, editor at large for *Christianity Today* and author of bestsellers such as *Pain: The Gift Nobody Wants* and *The Jesus I Never Knew*, lends his printed endorsement to the book's cover. While not openly condoning (or condemning) its conclusions, Yancey couldn't help but know that his praise of the book as "illuminating, challenging, disturbing and heart-wrenching" would make White's pro-gay philosophy more credible to evangelical readers.

8. Marsha Stevens, composer of "For Those Tears I Died" and one of the most influential gospel artists associated with the "Jesus movement," has discussed her belief that God sanctions her lesbian relationship in the *Los Angeles Times* ("Non-Traditional Churches Welcoming Gays to Flock," 21 June 1991, sec. B, p. 1) and details her transition from her former marriage to her association with the Metropolitan Community Church in Sylvia Pennington's *Ex-Gays? There Are None!* (Hawthorne: Lambda Christian Fellowship, 1989), pp. 365-92.

9. Tammy Faye Bakker, Jim Bakker's former wife and co-host of the "PTL Show," is (as of this writing) co-hosting a syndicated television show with openly gay Jim Bullock who describes himself as "Christian and Southern Baptist." By all accounts, Ms. Bakker still presents herself as a Christian public figure. "Tammy Faye's New Jim," *Out Magazine*, 6 February 1996, p. 34.

10. "4 Churches Expelled for Outreach to Gays," *Los Angeles Times*, 13 January 1996, sec. B, pp. 8-9.

11. Ken Medema is a reknowned composer and featured artist at numerous Christian events. His endorsement of the pro-gay viewpoint is documented in the video "Bitter Sisters/Suffering Sons" (1994) produced by His Way Ministries, P.O. Box 4005, Ottowa, Kansas 66067.

12. "Freezing Out the Salvation Army," *The Advocate*, 6 February 1996, p. 18.

13. "The Bishop, the Priest, and His Lover," *Out Magazine*, 6 February 1996, p. 96.

14. "Ordination Dilemma for LA Bishop," *Los Angeles Times*, 13 January 1996, sec. B, pp. 8-9.

15. *National and International Religion Report*, 1 November 1993; cited in *The Exodus Standard*, December 1993, vol. 10, no. 4, p. 11.

16. "Church and Society," *Time*, 24 June 1991, p. 49.

17. "Goings on Behind Bedroom Doors," *U.S. News and World Report*, 10 June 1991, vol. 110, no. 22, p. 63.
18. "Clinton's Church Hosts Gay Activist Event," *Lambda Report*, January 1996, vol. 3, no. 4, p. 1.
19. Victor Paul Furnish, *The Moral Teaching of Paul* (Nashville: Abingdon Press, 1979).
20. Interview with Ken Korver, pastor of Emmanuel Reformed Church of Paramount, California, 2 February 1996.
21. "New Head of Disciples of Christ Would Permit Gays in Ministry," *Los Angeles Times*, 31 July 1993, sec. B, p. 12.
22. "4 Churches Expelled," p. 9.
23. "Rethinking the Origins of Sins," *Orange County Register*, 15 May 1993, sec. 1, p. 28.
24. Ron Rhodes, *The Culting of America* (Eugene: Harvest House Publishers, 1994), p. 27.
25. "Non-Traditional Churches Welcoming Gays to Flock," p. 12.
26. *Penpoint Journal*, June 1991, vol. 2, no. 3, p. 1.
27. "Church and Society," p. 50.
28. Rhodes, p. 35.

Chapter 1: Why Bother?

1. Grant, George and Horne, Mark, *Legislating Immorality* (Chicago: Moody Press, 1993), pp. 165-70.
2. "Learning from Catholic's Change," *Out NOW!* 27 June 1995, vol. 3, no. 13, p. 15.
3. The Metropolitan Community Church is not unique in this respect. Statements and beliefs twice as alarming were expressed at the Re-Imaging Conference at Wichita in 1993, which was attended by women representing mainline churches from across the country. See "Earthquake in the Mainline," *Christianity Today*, 14 November 1994, vol. 38, no. 13.
4. Hank Hanegraaff, *Christianity in Crisis* (Eugene: Harvest House Publishers, 1993), p. 291.
5. "Non-Traditional Churches Welcoming Gays to Flock," *Los Angeles Times*, 21 June 1991, sec. B, p. 1.
6. Mel White, *Stranger at the Gate* (New York: Simon and Schuster, 1994), pp. 132-33.
7. Troy Perry, *Don't Be Afraid Anymore* (New York: St. Martins Press, 1990), p. 20.
8. Troy Perry, in *Dallas Voice*, 19 July 1989; cited in William Dannemeyer, *Shadow in the Land* (San Francisco: Ignatious Press, 1989), p. 101.
9. Grant and Horne, p. 172.
10. Ibid.
11. Pennington, *Ex-Gays? There Are None!* p. 161.
12. "Goings on Behind Bedroom Doors," *U.S. News and World Report*, 10 June 1991, vol. 110, no. 22, p. 63.
13. Perry, *Don't Be Afraid Anymore*, p. 340.
14. F. LaGard Smith, *Sodom's Second Coming* (Eugene: Harvest House Publishers, 1993), p. 130.
15. "Fallout Escalates Over Goddess Sophia," *Christianity Today*, 4 April 1994, p. 74; cited in Greg Laurie, *The Great Compromise*, p. 11.
16. "Earthquake in the Mainline," p. 40.
17. Ibid.

Chapter 2: Cultural Consequences

1. I realize there are non-Christian groups, both secular and religious, that also oppose the gay rights movement. I support and work with many of them. By

and large, however, I believe that most voices resisting this ideology come from Christians.

2. Some studies have led people to this conclusion, though. The Institute for the Scientific Study of Sexuality, for example, stated in 1984 that homosexuals were at least 12 times more likely to molest children than heterosexuals. (See Marlin Maddox, *Answers to the Gay Deception* [Dallas: International Christian Media, 1994], p. 62.) That may be. My doubts, though, stem from the definition of "homosexual" in these studies. If a man molests a boy, as I read in the American Psychiatric Association's *Diagnostic and Statistical Manual*, he is a pedophile (which involves sexual attraction to children) rather than a homosexual (which involves sexual attraction to adults of the same sex). Furthermore, adults who are sexually attracted to children are far more likely to molest children of the same sex, not because they are homosexual, but because they have more intimate access to children of their own sex (through bathrooms, gymnasiums, and so forth) than to children of the opposite sex. They, too, it seems to me, are pedophiles, not homosexuals.

3. Men referred to here are those who stayed in counseling for a minimum of six months. Many others have come for consultations or shorter counseling periods.

4. Ronald Bayer, *Homosexuality and American Psychiatry: The Politics of Diagnosis* (New York: Basic Books, 1981), p. 172.

5. Ibid., p. 119.

6. Kenneth Lewes, *The Psychoanalytic Theory of Male Homosexuality* (New York: Simon and Schuster, 1988), p. 222.

7. Ibid.

8. See Bayer, chapter 3, for a fascinating, detailed account of this.

9. "Pedophilia Not Always a Disorder?" *NARTH Bulletin*, April 1995, vol. 3, no. 1, p. 1.

10. "Pedophilia Steps into the Daylight," *Citizen Magazine*, 16 November 1992, vol. 6, no. 11, p. 6.

11. Ibid.

12. Ibid.

13. "Treating a Delicate Story of a Soldier and a Boy Tenderly," *New York Times*, May 7, 1993, sec. C, p.14.

14. John Money, quoted in *Paidika: The Journal of Pedophilia* (The Netherlands), 2:7, p. 5.

15. "Progress in Empirical Research on Children's Sexuality," *SIECUS Report*, 12:2, p. 2.

16. "Pedophilia Steps into the Daylight," p. 7.

17. Ibid.

18. Judith Reisman, *Kinsey, Sex and Fraud* (Lafayette: Huntington, 1990), p. 131.

19. "Cradle to Grave Intimacy," *Time*, September 1981, p. 69.

20. "Interview: John Money," *Paidika Journal*, 2:7, p. 9.

21. "Stonewall Celebrates 25 Years of 'Gay Rights'" *The Lambda Report*, July 1994, vol. 2, no. 3, p. 10.

22. Gregory King of the gay-oriented Human Rights Campaign Fund, for example, doesn't even consider NAMBLA to be a gay organization, whereas lesbian author Camille Paglia states, "It [pedophilia] has been at the center of gay male sex for thousands of years." Ibid.

23. Review the sins listed in Leviticus 20 and you might find a clue. Along those lines, a remark made by gay activist Sara Cohen at the Yale Annual ball is noteworthy: "What's wrong with a little bestiality?" Cited in Dinesh D'Souza, *Illiberal Education: The Politics of Race and Sex on Campus* (New York: Free Press, 1991), p. 12.

24. James Dobson, *Children at Risk* (Dallas: Word Publishing, 1990), p. 26.

25. Ibid., p. 25.

26. Ibid., p. 27.

27. From Project 10 brochure.
28. Ann Heron, *One Teenager in 10* (Boston: Alyson, 1983), pp. 60-62.
29. "Revolt in Queens," *The American Spectator,* February 1993, vol. 26, no. 2, p. 267.
30. Ibid., p. 30.
31. "Gay Activists Channel AIDS-Education Funds into Controversial Programs," *Southern California Christian Times,* January 1996, vol. 7, no. 1, p. 4.
32. Virginia Uribe, in the video "Gay Rights/Special Rights," Jeremiah Films, 1993. Available through TVC, 100 South Anaheim Blvd., Suite 250, Anaheim, CA 92805.
33. "One in 10," Youth Group Brochure, P.O. Box 26836, Albuquerque, New Mexico, 87125.
34. "Demography of Sexual Orientation in Adolescents," *Pediatrics: The Journal of the American Academy of Pediatrics,* April 1992, vol. 89.
35. June Reinische, *The Kinsey Institute New Report on Sex* (New York: St. Martin's Press, 1990), p. 138.
36. "Revolt in Queens," p. 29.
37. Ibid.
38. *Newsweek,* 19 September 1994, pp. 50-51; cited in *NARTH Bulletin,* December 1994, vol. 2, no. 3.
39. Ibid.
40. "Young Gays Straying Into Unsafe Sex," *Los Angeles Times,* 3 September 1995, sec. A, p. 3.
41. "AIDS Infection Highest Among Men 18 to 25," *Orange County Register,* 10 February 1996, sec. 1, p. 16.
42. "Gay Rights/Special Rights" video. Dobson also cites gay advocates allowing for bisexual or homosexual trios. See Dobson, p. 117.
43. Eric Buehrer, *The Public Orphanage* (Dallas: Word, 1995), p. 14.
44. Ibid., p. 15.
45. Dobson, p. 167.
46. Ibid., p. 168.
47. Dennis Praeger, "Why Judaism Rejected Homosexuality," *Mission and Ministry: The Quarterly Magazine of Trinity Episcopal School for Ministry,* Summer 1995, vol. 10, no. 3.
48. Ibid.

Chapter 3: How It Began: The Gay Rights Movement (1969-1979)

1. Dennis Praeger, in *Broward Jewish World,* 16 October 1990; cited in Grant, George and Horne, Mark, *Legislating Immorality* (Chicago: Moody Press, 1993), pp. 24-25.
2. See John Boswell, *Christianity, Social Tolerance and Homosexuality* (Chicago: University of Chicago Press, 1980), pp. 61-87; Grant and Horne, pp. 21-38; and Wainwright Churchill, *Homosexual Behavior Among Males* (New York: Hawthorne Books, 1967), pp. 121-41.
3. Ronald Bayer, *Homosexuality and American Psychiatry* (New York: Basic Books, 1981), p. 15.
4. Dennis Praeger, "Why Judaism Rejected Homosexuality," *Mission and Ministry: The Quarterly Magazine of Trinity Episcopal School for Ministry,* Summer 1995, vol. 10, no. 3, p. 13.
5. Kinsey in 1948, of course, and others. See Kenneth Lewes, *The Psychoanalytic Theory of Male Homosexuality* (New York: Simon and Schuster, 1988), pp. 48-122; and Bayer, pp. 68-69.
6. Bayer lists some organizations preexisting Mattachine, but cites Mattachine as the most important and, in retrospect, the most easily identifiable starting point.
7. Neil Miller, *Out of the Past: Gay and Lesbian History from 1869 to the Present* (New York: Vintage Books, 1995), pp. 333-44.
8. Bayer, p. 71.

9. Wood and Dietrich, *The AIDS Epidemic* (Portland: Multnomah, 1990), p. 75.
10. Ibid., p. 75; and Churchill, p. 293.
11. Bayer, p. 76.
12. Ibid., pp. 83-88.
13. Churchill, pp. 200, 293.
14. Bayer, p. 92.
15. Ibid.
16. Ibid., p. 93.
17. Quote from the *Dallas Voice*, 19 July 1989, p. 24; cited in William Dannemeyer, *Shadow in the Land* (San Francisco: Ignatious Press, 1989), p. 101.
18. Troy Perry, *Don't Be Afraid Anymore* (New York: St. Martin's Press, 1990), p. 7.
19. Ibid., p. 34.

Chapter 4: War: The Gay Rights Movement (1969–1979)

1. Leigh Rutledge, *The Gay Decades* (New York: Penguin Books, 1992), pp. 1-2. See also Martin Duberman's *Stonewall* (New York: Dutton, 1993) for a full treatment of the event.
2. Rutledge, p. 2.
3. Roger Biery, *Understanding Homosexuality: The Pride and the Prejudice* (Austin: Edward William Publishing Co., 1990), pp. 194-97. See also Rutledge, p. 7, for one of too many examples of this, in which a group of English youths beat a gay man to death with clubs as he was walking down the street in Wimbledon Common. "When you're hitting a queer," a proud young "fag basher" commented afterwards, "there's nothing to be scared of 'cause you know they won't go to the law."
4. Rutledge, pp. 98-99.
5. Ibid., p. 16.
6. Baird and Baird, *Homosexuality: Debating the Issues* (Amherst: Prometheus Books, 1995), p. 23.
7. This is not to suggest a favorable comparison between the civil rights movement and the gay rights movement, as I see the two as being fundamentally different (see chapter 7). But the militant gay power movement linked itself, both in its title and tactics, to the civil rights and black power movements, sometimes with, and sometimes without, their approval. (See Rutledge, p. 23.)
8. "Intimate Friendships," *U.S. News and World Report*, 5 July 1993, vol. 115, no. 1, p. 50.
9. Ibid.
10. See Baird and Baird; Ronald Bayer, *Homosexuality and American Psychiatry: The Politics of Diagnosis* (New York: Basic Books, 1981); Duberman; and Neil Miller, *Out of the Past: Gay and Lesbian History from 1869 to the Present* (New York: Vintage Books, 1995).
11. Some Christian bookstores order pro-gay books without knowing it. Many times I've found these materials in stores run by conservative Christians who wouldn't consider having the gay view promoted on their shelves. But the titles of the books (*Is the Homosexual My Neighbor? Christianity, Social Tolerance and Homosexuality, Can Homophobia Be Cured?*) are often innocent or compassionate sounding. When I've pointed this out to the owners, they've always removed the books, surprised to find they'd been peddling the gay ideology without realizing it.
12. Perry, *Don't Be Afraid Anymore*, p. 208.
13. Ibid., p. 211.
14. Ibid, pp. 183-85.
15. Ibid., pp. 185-87.
16. Ibid., p. 171.
17. William Dannemeyer *Shadow in the Land* (San Francisco: Ignatious Press, 1989), p. 104.

18. Mel White, *Stranger at the Gate* (New York: Simon and Schuster, 1994), p. 268.
19. Perry, *Don't Be Afraid Anymore*, p. 283.
20. Rutledge, p. 4.
21. Ibid., p. 47.
22. Ibid., p. 100. It is disturbing to note that nearly 20 years later (February 1996) a heresy trial within the Episcopal church is in progress over the ordination of a gay deacon. The bishops calling for the trial should be commended, of course. But why did it take Episcopalian leadership two decades to act on a problem that was out in the open back in 1977?
23. Isamu Yamamoto, *The Crisis of Homosexuality* (Wheaton: Victor Books, 1990), pp. 79-80.
24. Bayer, p. 204.
25. Ibid., pp. 156-59.
26. Ibid., pp. 156-57.
27. Ibid., p. 157.
28. Yamamoto, p. 49.
29. Anita Bryant, *The Anita Bryant Story* (Old Tappan: Fleming Revell, 1977).
30. Ibid., p. 79.
31. Biery, p. 201.
32. Perry, *Don't Be Afraid Anymore*, p. 140.
33. Bryant, p. 35.
34. Perry, *Don't Be Afraid Anymore*, p. 145.
35. Bayer, p. 155.
36. Perry, pp. 146-71.
37. White, p. 270.
38. Ibid., p. 146.
39. Rutledge, p. 140.
40. See Perry, *Don't Be Afraid Anymore*, p. 279, White pp. 291-96, and Rutledge, pp. 146, 186, 197.

Chapter 5: The Gay Christian Movement Comes of Age

1. Bailey, *Homosexuality and the Western Tradition* (Hambden, CT: Shoe String Books, Inc., 1975); Wainwright Churchill, *Homosexual Behavior Among Males* (New York: Hawthorne Books, 1967); and Horner, *Jonathan Loved David* (Philadelphia: Westminster Press, 1978); cf. Clinton Jones, *Homosexuality and Counseling* (Philadelphia: Fortress Press, 1974); John McNeil, *The Church and the Homosexual* (Kansas City: Sheed, Andrews and McMeel, 1976); Troy Perry, *The Lord Is My Shepherd and He Knows I'm Gay* (Los Angeles: Nash Publishing, 1972); Norman Pittinger, *Time for Consent* (London: SCM Press, 1970); Richard Woods, *Another Kind of Love* (Chicago: Thomas Moore Press, 1977).
2. A national group of pro-gay Bible studies and fellowships founded by New York psychotherapist Ralph Blair, Evangelicals Concerned, is probably the most theologically conservative of all the gay Christian groups and is the most articulate in defending the pro-gay theology.
3. See Paul Morrison, *Shadow of Sodom* (Wheaton: Tyndale House, 1978), p. 15, for one of many examples.
4. Anita Bryant, *The Anita Bryant Story* (Old Tappan: Fleming Revell, 1977), p. 35.
5. Troy Perry, *Don't Be Afraid Anymore* (New York: St. Martin's Press, 1990), p. 41.
6. An example: "Paul [the apostle] did not like homosexuals, but Paul did not take to women's rights . . . Not once did Jesus say, 'Come unto me all ye heterosexuals — No! Jesus said 'Come unto me all ye that labor and are heavy laden, and I will give you rest. And that includes homosexuals, too. God doesn't condemn me for a sex drive that He has created in me." See Perry, *The Lord Is My Shepherd*, pp. 150-51.
7. Horner, p. 98.

8. F. LaGard Smith, *Sodom's Second Coming* (Eugene: Harvest House Publishers, 1993), p. 120.
9. See chapter 7 for refutations to LeVay, Kinsey, and the APA.
10. If academic credentials prove what a person says is credible, then what are we to make of Angela Davis or Timothy Leary? Just a thought.
11. Leigh Rutledge, *The Gay Decades* (New York: Penguin Books, 1992), p. 170.
12. John Boswell, *Christianity, Social Tolerance and Homosexuality* (Chicago: University of Chicago Press, 1980), Preface, p. xv.
13. Elodie Ballantine Emig, "1 Corinthians 6:9—Part III," *Where Grace Abounds Newsletter,* P.O. Box 18871, Denver, CO 80218-0871.
14. Boswell, p. 117.
15. Thomas E. Schmidt, *Straight and Narrow? Compassion and Clarity in the Homosexual Debate* (Downers Grove: InterVarsity Press, 1995); and Marion Soards, *Scripture and Homosexuality: Biblical Authority and the Church Today* (Westminster: John Knox, 1995).
16. Perry, *Don't Be Afraid Anymore,* p. 233.
17. Ibid., p. 234.

Chapter 6: The Pro-Gay Theology

1. See Hank Hanegraaff, *Christianity in Crisis* (Eugene: Harvest House Publishers, 1993), p. 317, for the roles these creeds play in the essentials of Christianity.
2. Troy Perry, *Don't Be Afraid Anymore* (New York: St. Martins Press, 1990), p. 342.
3. Ibid., p. 339.
4. Randy Frame, "Seeking a Right to the Rite," *Christianity Today,* 4 March 1996, vol. 40, no. 3, p. 66.
5. Perry, *Don't Be Afraid Anymore,* p. 39.
6. Mel White, *Stranger at the Gate* (New York: Simon and Schuster, 1994), pp. 295, 300, 309, 315.
7. Scroogs, Robin, *The New Testament and Homosexuality* (Philadelphia: Fortress Press, 1983), p. 127.
8. Morris, p. 89.
9. Perry, *Don't Be Afraid Anymore,* p. 39.
10. White, pp. 36-39.
11. Ibid, p. 156.
12. Sylvia Pennington, *Ex-Gays? There Are None!* p. 388.

Chapter 7: Social Justice Arguments—Part One

1. Kirk, Marshall and Madsen, Hunter, *After the Ball: How America Will Conquer Its Fear and Hatred of Gays in the 90s* (New York: Doubleday, 1989). I've been amazed, since first reading Kirk and Madsen's book in 1989, how obviously they tipped their hand by publishing their strategies. Didn't they realize that conservative readers keep up on gay literature, just as gays regularly read our books and materials to keep up on what we're saying? At any rate, you'll find Kirk and Madsen quoted in countless conservative Christian books and articles as an example of gay tactics and dishonest strategies. I hope their community hasn't been too hard on them for giving the pro-gay battle plan away.
2. Thomas Schmidt, *Straight and Narrow? Compassion and Clarity in the Homosexuality Debate* (Downers Grove: InterVarsity Press, 1995), pp. 172-73.
3. Gebhard, Paul, *The Kinsey Data* (Philadelphia: Saunders Press, 1979), p. 23.
4. Bell, Alan and Weinberg, Martin, *Homosexualities: A Study of Diversities Among Men and Women* (New York: Simon and Schuster, 1978).
5. Ibid.
6. Randy Frame, "Seeking a Right to the Rite," *Christianity Today,* 4 March 1996, vol. 40, no. 3, p. 66.

7. Joseph Shapiro, "Straight Talk About Gays," *U.S. News and World Report*, 15 July 1993, vol. 115, no. 1, p. 48.
8. "Rethinking the Origins of Sin," *Los Angeles Times*, 15 May 1993, sec. A, p 31.
9. Shapiro, p. 48.
10. Simon LeVay, "A Difference in Hypothalamic Structure Between Heterosexual and Homosexual Men," *Science*, 30 August 1991, pp. 1034-37.
11. John Ankerberg, "The Myth that Homosexuality Is Due to Biological or Genetic Causes," (research paper), P.O. Box 8977, Cattanooga, TN 37411.
12. "Is This Child Gay?" *Newsweek*, 9 September 1991, p. 52.
13. Ibid.
14. *Los Angeles Times*, 16 September 1992, p. 1; cited in *NARTH Newsletter*, December 1992, p. 1.
15. "Sexual Disorientation: Faulty Research in the Homosexual Debate," *Family* (A publication of the Family Research Council), June 1992, p. 4, 700 13th St. NW Ste. 500, Washington, DC 20005.
16. "Is This Child Gay?" p. 52.
17. Quoted in *Los Angeles Times*, 30 August 1991, sec. A, p. 1.
18. Quoted in *Time*, 9 September 1991, vol. 138, no. 10, p. 61.
19. Quoted in *Newsweek*, 9 September 1991, p. 52.
20. "Gay Genes Revisited," *Scientific American*, November 1995, p. 26.
21. Bailey, Michael and Pillard, Richard, "A Genetic Study of Male Sexual Orientation," Archives of General Psychiatry, 1991, no. 48, pp. 1089-96.
22. David Gelman, "Born or Bred?" *Newsweek*, 24 February 1992, p. 46
23. Ibid.
24. Ibid.
25. King and McDonald, "Homosexuals Who Are Twins," *The British Journal of Psychiatry*, March 1992, vol. 160, p. 409.
26. Dean Hamer, "A Linkage Between DNA Markers on the X Chromosome and Male Sexual Orientation," *Science*, 16 July 1993, no. 261, pp. 321-27.
27. "Gay Genes Revisited: Doubts Arise over Research on the Biology of Homosexuality," *Scientific American*, November 1995, p. 26.
28. Ibid.
29. Frank Siexas, former director of the National Council on Alcoholism; quoted in Dannemeyer, p. 55.
30. Joe Dallas, "Born Gay?" *Christianity Today*, 22 June 1992, p. 22; *Chronicle of Higher Education*, 5 February 1992, p. A7.
31. "Rethinking the Origins of Sin," p. 31.
32. Robert Wright, "Our Cheating Hearts," *Time*, 15 August 1994, vol. 144, no. 7 pp. 44-52.
33. *Chronicle of Higher Education*, 5 February 1992, p. A7.
34. Ibid.
35. Ibid.
36. Ibid.
37. Richard Isay, interviewed on "Gays and the Church," "ABC World News Tonight," 28 February 1996.
38. Richard Isay, *Being Homosexual* (New York: Farrar, Straus, Giroux, 1989), p. 112.
39. Mel White, *Stranger at the Gate* (New York: Simon and Schuster, 1994), p. 5
40. Perry, *Don't Be Afraid Anymore*, p. 64.
41. Scanzoni and Mollenkott, p. 107.
42. Sylvia Pennington, *Ex-Gays? There Are None!* p. 108.
43. Schmidt, p. 155.
44. Bell and Weinberg.
45. Ruben Fine, *Psychoanalytic Theory, Male and Female Homosexuality: Psychological Approaches*, Louis Diamant, ed. (New York: Hemisphere, 1987), pp. 84-86.

46. Irving Bieber, *Homosexuality: A Psychoanalytic Study* (New York: Basic Books, 1962), pp. 318-19.
47. Masters and Johnson, *Homosexuality in Perspective* (Boston: Little Brown and Company, 1979), p. 402.
48. Wood and Dietrich, *The AIDS Epidemic* (Portland: Multnomah, 1990), p. 238.
49. June Reinisch, *The New Kinsey Report* (New York: St Martin's Press, 1990), pp. 138, 143.
50. Stanton Jones, "The Loving Opposition," *Christianity Today*, 19 July 1993, vol. 37, no. 8, cited in Baird, p. 252.
51. Ronald Bayer, *Homosexuality and American Psychiatry: The Politics of Diagnosis* (New York: Basic Books, 1981), p. 39.
52. Ibid., p. 40.
53. Ibid., pp. 99-126.
54. Ibid., p. 142.
55. Ibid., p. 148.
56. Ibid., p. 159-62.
57. Scanzoni and Mollenkott, pp. 111-12; Biery, p. 185.
58. Bayer, pp. 3-4.
59. Ibid., p. 128.
60. Ibid., p. 167.
61. Kinsey, Alfred, *Sexual Behavior in the Human Male* (Philadelphia: Saunders Press, 1948), p. 625.
62. Ibid., p. 638.
63. Reinisch, p. 138.
64. Judith Reisman, *Kinsey, Sex and Fraud* (Lafayette: Huntington, 1990), p. 9.
65. Lesbian activist with ACT-UP, interviewed in "Gay Rights-Special Rights" video.
66. Stanton Jones, "The Loving Opposition," *Christianity Today*, 19 July 1993, reprinted in Baird and Baird, *Homosexuality: Debating the Issues* (Amherst: Prometheus Books, 1995), p. 253.

Chapter 8: Social Justice Arguments—Part Two
1. Joseph Shapiro, "Straight Talk About Gays," *U.S. News and World Report*, 15 July 1993, vol. 115, no. 1, p. 42.
2. Richard Isay, *Being Homosexual* (New York: Farrar, Straus, Giroux, 1989), p. 145.
3. Joseph Nicolosi, *Reparative Therapy of Male Homosexuality* (Northvale: Jason Aaronson, 1991), p. 138.
4. Mel White, *Stranger at the Gate* (New York: Simon and Schuster, 1994), p. 307.
5. Andrew Sullivan, *Virtually Normal: An Argument About Homosexuality* (New York: Alfred Knopf, 1995), pp. 21-22. Sullivan shows courage in promoting a view that will surely raise hackles in some gay circles, but he represents the more moderate gays who, I believe, are more common than the strident ones getting the most attention these days.
6. Roger Biery, *Understanding Homosexuality: The Pride and the Prejudice* (Austin: Edward William Publishing Co., 1990), p. 201.
7. White, p. 236.
8. Ibid.
9. John Boswell, *Christianity, Social Tolerance and Homosexuality* (Chicago: University of Chicago Press, 1980), p. vii.
10. Biery, p. 126.
11. John Anderson, "Breaking the Silence: Creating Safe Schools for Gay Youth," *Student Assistance Journal*, March/April 1994, p. 1.
12. "Homosexual Public School Program Gains APS Favor," *Citizens for Excellence in Education Awareness Bulletin*, October 1992.

244 A Strong Delusion

13. Peter LaBarbera, "Gay Youth Suicide: Myth Is Used to Promote Homosexual Agenda," p. 9. Available through LAMBDA Report, P.O. Box 45252, Washington, DC 20026-5252.
14. Ibid., p. 3.
15. Ibid.
16. Ibid., p. 5.
17. Ibid., p. 7.
18. "Homosexuals Can Change," *Christianity Today*, 16 February 1981, p. 37.

Chapter 9: General Religious Arguments
1. Mel White, *Stranger at the Gate* (New York: Simon and Schuster, 1994), p. 214.
2. George Barna, *What Americans Believe* (Ventura: Regal Books, 1991), p. 36; cited in Ron Rhodes, *The Culting of America* (Eugene: Harvest House Publishers, 1994), p. 23.
3. Stephen Lang, "Is Ignorance Bliss?" *Moody*, January/February 1996, vol. 96, no. 5, p. 13.
4. Charles Colson, excerpt from *The Body*; in *Christianity Today*, 23 November 1992, p. 29.
5. Elliot Miller, *A Crash Course on the New Age Movement* (Grand Rapids: Baker Book House, 1993), p. 16.
6. Cornelius Plantinga, "Natural Born Sinners," *Christianity Today*, 14 November 1994, vol. 38, no. 13, p. 25.
7. Lang, p. 13.
8. Troy Perry, *Don't Be Afraid Anymore* (New York: St. Martin's Press, 1990), p. 40.
9. White, p. 268.
10. Roger Biery, *Understanding Homosexuality: The Pride and the Prejudice* (Austin: Edward William Publishing Co., 1990), p. 138.
11. "Gays and the Church," "ABC World News Tonight," 28 February 1996.
12. Biery, pp. 176, 12.
13. White, p. 314.
14. For a fuller treatment of the "change" issue, and what sort of changes can be expected in treatment for homosexuality, see my book *Desires in Conflict* (Eugene: Harvest House Publishers, 1991).
15. Letter from Robertson to White cited in "Gay Crusade," *Orange County Register*, 6 July 1993, sec. 6, p. 1.

Chapter 10: The Nature and Use of the Bible
1. Stanton Jones, "The Loving Opposition," *Christianity Today*, 19 July 1993, vol. 37, no. 8, pp. 18-25.
2. Ramey and Mollenkott, p. 71.
3. Roger Biery, *Understanding Homosexuality: The Pride and the Prejudice* (Austin: Edward William Publishing Co., 1990), p. 146.
4. Mel White, *Stranger at the Gate* (New York: Simon and Schuster, 1994), p. 305.
5. "Straight Talk About Gays," *U.S. News and World Report*, 10 June 1991, p. 63.
6. "Gays and the Church," "ABC World News Tonight," 28 February 1996.
7. Joseph Gudel, "That Which Is Unnatural," *Christian Research Journal*, Winter 1993, vol. 15, no. 3, p. 12.
8. Perry, *Don't Be Afraid Anymore*, p. 339.
9. Ramey and Mollenkott, p. 1.
10. Just as the pro-life movement has its lunatic fringe, who call for the death of abortionists, so there are a few (very few, thank God) who really would advocate violence against gays. They are clearly a minority; it would be just as unfair to hold them up as typical conservative as it would be to hold the wildest gay activists up as typical of all gays and lesbians
11. Biery, p. 143.

12. John Boswell, *Christianity, Social Tolerance and Homosexuality* (Chicago: University of Chicago Press, 1980), p. 335.
13. Ballentine, "1 Corinthians 6:9—Part III."
14. Francis Schaeffer, *The Great Evangelical Disaster* (Westchester: Crossway Books, 1984), p. 151.
15. Thomas E. Schmidt, *Straight and Narrow? Compassion and Clarity in the Homosexual Debate* (Downers Grove: InterVarsity Press, 1995), p. 60.
16. Mollenkott, p. 125.
17. Troy Perry, *The Lord Is My Shepherd and He Knows I'm Gay* (Los Angeles: Nash Publishing, 1972), pp. 150-51.
18. Troy Perry, *Don't Be Afraid Anymore* (New York: St. Martin's Press, 1990), p. 39.
19. White, p. 305.
20. Scanzoni and Mollenkott, Preface, p. xi.
21. Perry, *Don't Be Afraid Anymore*, p. 140.
22. White, p. 311.

Chapter 11: Scriptural Arguments
1. Schmidt, p. 41.
2. Jones, p. 22.
3. Boswell, pp. 93-94.
4. Ramey and Mollenkott, pp. 57-58.
5. Ibid.
6. Schmidt, pp. 88-89.
7. Bruce Metzger, "What Does the Bible Have to Say About Homosexuality?" *Presbyterians for Renewal*, May 1993, p. 7.
8. Boswell, p. 100.
9. Perry, *Don't Be Afraid Anymore*, p. 341.
10. Boswell, p. 109.
11. Ramey and Mollenkott, pp. 65-66.
12. Perry, *Don't Be Afraid Anymore*, p. 342.
13. Schmidt, pp. 78-79.

Chapter 12: Confronting the Gay Christian Movement
1. Cal Thomas, "Religious Wing Has Too Much Faith In Caesar," *Los Angeles Times*, 21 March 1995, sec. B, p. 9.
2. "Gays and the Church," "ABC World News Tonight," 28 February 1996.
3. "The Homosexual Movement," cited in Baird and Baird, *Homosexuality: Debating the Issues* (Amherst: Prometheus Books, 1995), p. 34.
4. "Bitter Sisters/Suffering Sons" (video), His Way Ministries, 1994.
5. A survey conducted by the Media Research Center in 1993 found 150 stories on "pro-life intimidation" of abortion clinics; no reporting was found on this extreme San Francisco demonstration at Hamilton Square.
6. Cal Thomas, "Gay Scientists Can Count on Compliant Media," *NARTH Newsletter*, December 1995, vol. 3, no. 3, p. 17.
7 Roger Biery, *Understanding Homosexuality: The Pride and the Prejudice* (Austin: Edward William Publishing Co., 1990), p. 174.
8. *Christianity Today*, 14 August 1995, p. 25.

Chapter 13: Beyond Delusion
1. Francis Schaeffer, *The Great Evangelical Disaster* (Westchester: Crossway Books, 1984), p. 160.
2. Mel White, *Stranger at the Gate* (New York: Simon and Schuster, 1994), p. 317.
3. Troy Perry, quoted in Morris, p. 29.
4. *Time*, 24 June 1991.

Other Good Harvest House Reading

DESIRES IN CONFLICT
by *Joe Dallas*

Through Exodus International and Genesis Counseling, Joe Dallas counsels and trains others to work with identity problems associated with homosexuality. This book offers information, biblical counsel...and HOPE!

THE BONDAGE BREAKER
by *Neil T. Anderson*

Enslaved to negative thoughts, irrational feelings, or habitual sin? Understand the strategy of Satan and gain victory in your circumstances. Discusses the position and vulnerability of the believer, and steps to freedom in Christ.